# Positive Politics at Work

D. DOUGLAS McKENNA

JEFFREY J. McHENRY

The Business Skills Express Series



BUSINESS ONE IRWIN/MIRROR PRESS
Burr Ridge, Illinois
New York, New York
Boston, Massachusetts

| | |
|---|---|
| Mirror Press: | David R. Helmstadter<br>Carla F. Tishler |
| Editor-in-chief: | Jeffrey A. Krames |
| Project editor: | Rebecca Dodson |
| Production manager: | Laurie Kersch |
| Designer: | Jeanne M. Rivera |
| Art coordinator: | Heather Burbridge |
| Illustrator: | Boston Graphics, Inc. |
| Compositor: | Alexander Graphics |
| Typeface: | 12/14 Criterion |
| Printer: | Malloy Lithographing, Inc. |

**Library of Congress Cataloging-in-Publication Data**

McKenna, D. Douglas
Positive politics at work / D. Douglas McKenna and Jeffrey J. McHenry.
p. cm.
ISBN 1-55623-879-7
1. Politics, Practical. I. McHenry, Jeffrey J. II. Title.
JF2051.M395 1994
324.7—dc20 93–24062

*Printed in the United States of America*
1 2 3 4 5 6 7 8 9 0 ML 0 9 8 7 6 5 4 3

# PREFACE

Are you tired of all the politicking in your workplace? Do you find yourself asking, "Why can't we solve our problems without all the posturing and maneuvering!" If so, then this book is for you. This book should persuade you that participating in the political process is mandatory if you are going to get things done in your organization.

The ideas and exercises in this book will help you to make sense of the politics taking place in your organization right now. To accomplish this, the book will teach you how to

- make sense of workplace politics and your current political challenges.
- recognize the different strategies that shape your own and others' political actions.
- deal with people in a way that produces satisfying results in an efficient manner and builds good working relationships.
- work successfully with people who use negative political tactics.

A word of warning: the political process in organizations speeds up and slows down, but it never comes to a complete stop. While you are reading this book, people with political savvy and energy are working hard to further their own interests—perhaps for the good of all, but perhaps not. If you do not jump into the fray, you cannot defend or advance anyone's interests—not even your own. Let's get started now and keep ahead of the game.

D. Douglas McKenna
Jeffrey J. McHenry

# ABOUT THE AUTHORS

D. Douglas McKenna is General Manager, Human Resources Strategy and Services, for Microsoft Corporation. Dr. McKenna specializes in real-world solutions to issues of leadership and organizational development with a special concentration on preparing young leaders for executive-level responsibilities. Dr. McKenna is a writer and active participant in the Society for Industrial/Organizational Psychology and the Academy of Management. He is Professor of Management in the School of Business and Economics at Seattle Pacific University.

Jeffrey J. McHenry is an experienced consultant with leading software and professional service firms in the Pacific Northwest. His clients have included Microsoft, Boeing, and Weyerhaeuser. Dr. McHenry specializes in guiding human resources departments to be responsive to the strategic business challenges facing organizations. In his consulting work, Dr. McHenry focuses on diversity, teamwork, employee participation, and creating a work environment that encourages employees to reach their optimum potential. Dr. McHenry is on the executive committee of the Society of Industrial/Organizational Psychology (STOP) and a member of the Academy of Management. He is currently Associate Professor of Management in the School of Business and Economics at Seattle Pacific University.

# About Business One Irwin

Business One Irwin is the nation's premier publisher of business books. As a Times Mirror company, we work closely with Times Mirror training organizations, including Zenger-Miller, Inc., Learning International, Inc., and Kaset International to serve the training needs of business and industry.

**About the Business Skills Express Series**

This expanding series of authoritative, concise, and fast-paced books delivers high-quality training on key business topics at a remarkably affordable cost. The series will help managers, supervisors, and front-line personnel in organizations of all sizes and types hone their business skills while enhancing job performance and career satisfaction.

Business Skills Express books are ideal for employee seminars, independent self-study, on-the-job training, and classroom-based instruction. Express books are also convenient-to-use references at work.

# CONTENTS

# Self-Assessment

How effective are you at playing positive politics at work? This simple self-assessment will help you find out. Regardless of your final score, *Positive Politics at Work* will help you to reduce your political liabilities and increase your political assets.

Rate yourself on each of the ten items below using the following scale:

| | Almost Always | Some-times | Almost Never |
|---|---|---|---|
| 1. I am able to influence the opinions, attitudes, and actions of the people with whom I work. | ______ | ______ | ______ |
| 2. I am good at working through conflicts and disagreements with others. | ______ | ______ | ______ |
| 3. I have good relationships with the influential people in my office or workplace. | ______ | ______ | ______ |
| 4. I stand up for the things I care about at work. | ______ | ______ | ______ |
| 5. I work hard to understand the needs, interests, and concerns of others. | ______ | ______ | ______ |
| 6. I am open to others' suggestions and ideas for resolving disagreements. | ______ | ______ | ______ |
| 7. When things get tense, I express my emotions without losing my cool. | ______ | ______ | ______ |
| 8. When others will be affected by my actions, I tell them what I am going to do before I do it. | ______ | ______ | ______ |
| 9. When I have a problem with someone, I speak with him or her directly rather than talk with a third party about the problem. | ______ | ______ | ______ |
| 10. I can be counted on to do what I say I will do. | ______ | ______ | ______ |

CHAPTER

# 1 Politics: People Working Together

**This chapter will help you to:**

- Recognize politics at work.
- Distinguish positive from negative politics.

## Politics at Work

When you go out for lunch, chat in the hall with co-workers after meetings, or tell your spouse and friends about what is happening at work, what do you talk about? Do any of these topics sound familiar?

- "Have you heard that our department is going to be reorganized, AGAIN?!"
- "Do you think manufacturing will be able to pressure engineering into making those design changes?"
- "I can't believe David was promoted. All he's ever been good at is telling the right people what they want to hear."

This is the wonderful world of workplace politics. ■

**Workplace politics** is the continuous stream of interactions in which people try to get what they want by attempting to influence workplace decisions, events, and results. This definition of workplace politics probably includes many, if not most, of your everyday work interactions. In fact, there is very little that goes on in an organization that is not political in some way.

Think for a moment about the last time you were involved in writing or changing a job description, setting up employee work schedules or assignments for the week, or preparing an agenda for a staff meeting. No doubt these activities were political in some way.

Why are politics so much a part of our everyday life in organizations? The answer is deceptively simple. Organizations are made up of people—people who have similar and different goals, needs, aspirations, fears, values, beliefs, and perceptions. The differences in what they care about lead to disagreements about what to do, when to do it, how to do it, who will get what resources or rewards, and so on.

Some people are more politically active than others. We often think of "political people" as selfish, but they are not necessarily so. They may be politically active on behalf of other people or the organization as a whole. Regardless of the scope of their interests, politically active people are shaping what happens in and around your organization. When you are not politically active, you leave the fate of your interests and goals in the hands of those who are willing to take the time and energy required to play the influence game.

## Exercise 1.1

Think of five people you work with on a regular basis. Using the six spaces below, rank order these people *and yourself* in terms of how much time and energy each one spends trying to influence the thoughts, beliefs, decisions, and actions of others. Write the name of the "most politically active" person in the first spot and continue on down the list. Remember, the most politically active person is not necessarily the most influential, but rather is the one who invests the most time, energy, and resources in trying to influence what happens in your organization.

**1.** ____________________

**2.** ____________________

**3.** ____________________

**4.** ____________________

**5.** ____________________

**6.** ____________________

# POSITIVE VERSUS NEGATIVE POLITICS

**Politics are inevitable and even necessary in human organizations. But they can be played in ways that are constructive or destructive. Consider the following scenario.**

Susan Ranieri dropped by Ian Forbes' office right after a staff meeting. "Can you believe how George Marlin kisses up to the Product Development people?" she asked. "I can't believe he'd actually let them push their development schedule back three weeks if he didn't have a hidden agenda. He's obviously after that product manager spot that everyone is saying will open up next month. This delay is going to destroy our marketing plan. The sales manager will be furious when she hears about it." Ian nodded his head in earnest agreement, saying, "We've got to figure out how to block this change." ■

## Exercise 1.2

Think about the "politics" of the preceding vignette. Answer the following questions, using the definition of workplace politics on page 1.

1. What is George trying to do? How is his behavior political?

______________________________

______________________________

______________________________

2. What is Susan trying to do? How is her behavior political?

______________________________

______________________________

______________________________

3. What is Ian trying to do? How is his behavior political?

______________________________

______________________________

______________________________

George, Susan, and Ian are trying to influence the actions or decisions of others to serve their own goals, needs, or interests. George apparently wants to influence Product Development to choose him as the new product manager. Susan wants to influence Ian's attitude toward George and Ian's beliefs about the likely consequences of the schedule delay. She is trying to get Ian to see things her way and to gain an ally. Ian joins with Susan, apparently thinking that forming an alliance with her will serve his interests. Unfortunately, the way Susan and Ian are going about it—behind George's back—is likely to damage their relationship with George both in the short and long run. Imagine George's reaction when he finds out that Susan and Ian are meeting covertly to question his motives and to plan a way to undermine his efforts.

## Exercise 1.3

What do you think George will tell his wife about Susan and Ian if he discovers through the grapevine what they are doing?

____________________________________________________________

____________________________________________________________

There is a wiser, more constructive way to be involved in workplace politics than that demonstrated in the first scenario. Susan could have taken the following different approach.

Susan was floored in the meeting with Product Development (PD) when her marketing colleague George did not put up any resistance to PD's proposal that the development schedule be pushed back three weeks. Since this change would create serious timing and credibility problems for the sales force, Susan asked the group for a short break before they made a final decision on the schedule delay. Once outside the room, Susan pulled George and Ian into another conference room. "George," she said, "You're our leader on this product and I want to support you in the meeting. However, you must know that I will speak up against this schedule change if you don't. I'd like to avoid this if possible, because it will appear that our marketing team can't get its act together. So before I do that, I really want to hear your reasons for not opposing the delay." ■

Susan is still playing politics—she's trying to influence George to do what she wants. But consider how her approach is different this time and how it is likely to affect George.

## Exercise 1.4

1. How is Susan's second approach different from her first approach?

   ___

   ___

   ___

2. When he gets home at night, what do you think George will tell his wife about Susan and her new approach?

   ___

   ___

   ___

George probably will be unhappy with Susan in both cases (and eventually unhappy with Ian). But if Susan approaches him directly, he will know that he can count on her to tell him what she is thinking and be open to hearing his side of the story.

George's opinion of Susan is only one part of the story, however. Two other opinions of Susan need to be considered:

1. **Susan's opinion of herself.** If Susan takes the second approach, she can go home at night knowing that she was honest and direct with George. She will feel good about herself. And she will not have to worry about word of any covert actions getting back to George and creating even more conflict.
2. **Ian's opinion of Susan.** If Susan talks to Ian behind George's back, what assurance does Ian have that she will not do the same to him if it suits her interests in some future scenario? By dealing straight with George, Susan builds Ian's confidence that she will do the same with him, even when they disagree. Her reputation as an assertive but trustworthy partner grows.

Susan's second approach is an example of *positive politics*. To play positive politics, you must act in ways that produce **results and relationships:**

- You produce good *results* by using your power and influence to emphasize your goals, needs, interests, beliefs, and values.
- You produce *relationships* by considering other people's perspectives and interests and by building your reputation as a fair and reliable person.

When you behave in ways that do not produce results and relationships, over time you will sabotage yourself. You will be frustrated and unhappy, and you will not be able to count on others to defend your interests.

If you fail to build relationships, eventually you will sabotage your ability to realize any of your goals or interests that require the cooperation of other people. A reputation as a selfish, uncooperative, or unreliable partner will render you ineffective and helpless in most organizations. If this is the case, you become a victim of your own *negative politics.*

## Exercise 1.5

To apply the distinction between positive and negative politics, think about yourself and the same five co-workers you ranked in Exercise 1.1. How *generally* effective are each of these people in (1) achieving results they care about and (2) building strong working relationships with others?

1. ______________________________
2. ______________________________
3. ______________________________
4. ______________________________
5. ______________________________
6. ______________________________

In doing this exercise you may have found it hard to classify yourself or your co-workers *in general.* Your ability to get the results you want and build good working relationships often varies across situations and people. If this is true for you, then your goal should be to increase the amount of time you spend achieving results and building strong working relationships.

# Chapter Checkpoints

✓ Every organization is political. The critical issue is whether the politics in your workplace are positive or negative.

✓ Workplace politicians try to influence each other and events in ways that further their interests.

✓ Positive politics require that you achieve the results you want while building effective working relationships for the future.

CHAPTER

# 2 Political Challenges

**This chapter will help you to:**

- Know where to look for political action in an organization.
- Identify a number of current politically hot situations or challenges in your own organization.
- Choose your political battles wisely.
- Identify a high-priority political challenge to which you can immediately apply the ideas in this book.

## COMMON POLITICAL SITUATIONS

It is probably not hard to find political action in your organization. But there may be much more going on than you know. Listed below are the kinds of decisions that commonly stimulate politics in the workplace. Take a moment to think about each type of decision.

- **Deciding who gets to participate in what.** Example: Patty Renssler and her three direct reports decided to exclude the rest of the 14-member marketing staff from the three-day strategic planning meeting offsite because the rest of the group "didn't have a broad enough perspective on the business" to be helpful.

- **Deciding who gets what information.** Example: Ever since the new group manager was hired, Sam Rollins has found himself left "out of the loop." No one stops by his office anymore to keep him posted on what is happening. He is regularly left out of meetings he previously led.

- **Deciding who is responsible for what.** Example: Writers and editors are at war over who has the final call on ad copy before it goes to production.

- **Deciding who gets what resources (budget, head count, facilities, time).** Example: Vanessa Washington learned that there was an opening for one more employee to attend the training conference in Dallas. She knew that several other departments would try to fill the opening with one of their employees, so she immediately went to the vice president's office and obtained his approval for her administrative assistant, Michael Jarvis, to attend the conference.

- **Making staffing decisions (hiring, discipline, termination, promotions, demotions, pay).** Example: "The only reason Ralph Sturgis got that promotion instead of me," Ryan Benson complained, "was because he goes golfing with the boss and I don't."

- **Determining who gets credit or blame.** Example: Angela Columbo listed herself as the sole author of her work team's marketing analysis of a proposed new toy line. Then, before any of the other team members had even seen the report, she sent a copy to all of the senior managers in sales, marketing, and product development—including the president of the company.

- **Coordinating related activities across people or groups (making schedules, assigning costs, making handoffs).** Example: Petros Katz left a voicemail message for Sarah Chase saying that Sarah would have to handle the press release due tomorrow because he had been unable to get it done in the last two weeks. He was calling from the airport, heading for his vacation to Mazatlan.

- **Changing just about anything to which a person or group is accustomed.** Example: The new general manager was caught completely by surprise by the uproar the reorganization seemed to create. She had never heard so much complaining or seen so much cutthroat scrambling for power.

What makes these decisions politically potent? They all have a high potential for conflict of interest. People are likely to think that they are not getting something they care about or that something they do care about is at risk.

## Exercise 2.1

Write examples from your own recent experience in which the decisions outlined above have generated political heat and conflict of interest in your organization.

**Participation:** ______________________________

______________________________

______________________________

**Information:** ______________________________

______________________________

______________________________

**Responsibilities:** ______________________________

______________________________

______________________________

**Resources:** ______________________________

______________________________

______________________________

**Staffing:** ______________________________

______________________________

______________________________

**Credit/Blame:** ______________________________________________

______________________________________________

______________________________________________

**Coordination:** ______________________________________________

______________________________________________

______________________________________________

**Change:** ______________________________________________

______________________________________________

______________________________________________

Now that you have had a chance to think about the range of political situations and activity occurring in your workplace, take a look at a "who's responsible for what" clash between two people in different departments. See if the underlying interests and concerns driving the conflict sound familiar.

**Shipping and the Surly Sales Representative: Part I**

Chris Farley is a supervisor in the shipping department. Lately, she has been having a lot of problems with Charlie Kantrovitz, who is one of the company's top sales representatives.

Charlie refuses to complete paperwork during the week. Each night Charlie calls in and leaves a voicemail message detailing all of the orders he has received that day, even though company policy prohibits shipments without a completed order form signed by a sales rep. Charlie's messages are often rambling, and it is difficult for Juan Morales—Chris's shipping clerk—to record and fill the orders accurately. Juan often calls Charlie for help, but Charlie is rarely in his office, and it usually takes him two to three days to return Juan's calls.

When Chris asked Charlie for better cooperation, he refused. "I'm too busy selling to run the shipping department. Who do you think brings in the money around here? Just once I'd like a little appreciation from you folks in shipping. If it wasn't for sales reps like me, there'd be no money to pay those whining crybabies working for you!"

Recently, many customers have complained about delayed orders and errors in shipments, so Chris is feeling pressured by her manager, Eric Stavros, to improve her unit's performance. Deanna Smythe—Charlie's manager—has complained to Eric several times about the shipping problems and has asked if she can help improve the situation, but Eric has never asked Deanna for better cooperation from Charlie. And Chris is not sure if Eric has enough clout to pressure Deanna or Charlie to cooperate. After all, the company would never fire Charlie—its top sales representative—just because he does not like paperwork.



"It would be a lot easier for the company to replace a shipping supervisor than it would be to replace a star sales rep," Chris thinks to herself. She feels powerless. She wonders, "How should I approach this situation?" ■

Each of the players in this situation has personal concerns at stake. Chris is concerned about:

- Satisfying and keeping customers.
- Making sure that her department meets its objectives.
- Getting a good performance review from her boss.
- Minimizing the time it takes to work her problem out with Charlie.
- Preventing Charlie from submarining her reputation in the company.

Charlie also has interests and concerns—some similar and some different from Chris's:

- Satisfying and keeping customers.
- Making sure he meets his sales goals.
- Keeping his freedom to do his job the way he wants to do it.
- Maximizing his time spent selling, and minimizing his time spent on administrative tasks.

At this point, it looks as though Charlie is in the driver's seat because he is stonewalling Chris's requests. His interests—as he sees the situation now—are best served by keeping things the same. And he has been very successful so far.

Chris, on the other hand, is unable to get what she needs from the present situation. She wants and needs Charlie to make a change. So far her attempts to influence him have been somewhat tentative—a single conversation with Charlie and a request to her boss to talk with Charlie's manager. It looks like Chris has doubts about her ability to be politically successful in this situation. What should she do? Is this a battle worth fighting? How much energy should she invest in trying to turn this situation around, particularly when there are other fires burning?



## CHOOSING YOUR POLITICAL BATTLES

Playing politics takes time and energy. You need to think carefully about where to invest your limited time and energy for maximum political benefit. Choosing your battles is always a matter of judgment, but you can improve your judgment by asking yourself the following questions:

1. Am I getting results?
2. What are my interests and are they at stake?
3. How likely is it that I can succeed in getting what I need?
4. How good are my working relationships with the people involved?
5. What is the priority of this particular battle?

### Am I Getting Results?

If what you are doing now is not producing the results you want, then it is time to do something different. This may mean escalating your investment, changing your strategy, or even giving up the battle.

It is pretty clear that Chris's approach to influencing Charlie has not yet worked. She needs to do something different.

### What Are My Interests and Are They at Stake?

You cannot play positive politics without having a good handle on what you need to feel satisfied and fulfilled. Your interests are different from what you simply want, desire, or fear. Your "wants" will make your life easier, happier, or more satisfying today. Your "interests" will help you reach your long-term goals and feel good about yourself. One way to distinguish between your wants and your interests is to use the "three-month test." Looking back on a current political battle three months from now, what will you say was at stake? What will you wish you had done? Will you have regrets if you fail to take action today? If the answer to this last question is "yes," then your interests are at stake and you must act now.

Chris has a number of very important interests at stake. In particular, Charlie's actions are hurting her unit's ability to satisfy customers and her performance as a manager. These are priorities she cares about in the long term, so she must make sure her interests are satisfied.

## How Likely Is It That I Can Succeed in Getting What I Need?

Do not fight battles that you are likely to lose unless you have no other way of defending or achieving your interests. If you continually find yourself on the losing end of political battles, you must develop new sources of power or move to another situation where the power you have will get you what you need.

In Chris's case, it is not clear that she will be successful in influencing Charlie to behave differently. As the manager of a cost center, she may have a hard time convincing a revenue producer such as Charlie to change his ways. And Chris's boss seems to have little power or willingness to help. Nevertheless, Chris might have some sources of power that she has not yet put into play. For example, the fact that customers are complaining may provide her with some leverage in negotiating a deal with Charlie. She also might create a simpler way for Charlie to pass his orders accurately, thus satisfying both their interests.

## How Good Are My Working Relationships with the People Involved?

Every political interaction takes time and energy—some a lot more than others. To predict how much time and energy you will need to produce a favorable result, consider the quality of your working relationship with the people involved: the better your relationship, the less time and energy are needed.

In Chris's case, her working relationship with Charlie is not particularly strong. Charlie does not seem to care about Chris's problems and his stonewalling is chewing up a lot of her time. If she continues to bug him about the problem and escalates it to higher-level management, however, she may cost Charlie more time than the problem is worth.

## What Is the Priority of This Particular Battle?

It is easy to fall into the illusion that everything is critical. Can you really do it all? Is it necessary? Is this really your problem? You should concentrate your efforts on those situations that are *directly* related to achieving your real interests.

Processing customer orders in a timely, accurate fashion is the mission of Chris's department. It is hard to imagine another political issue that would be more important to Chris than this one.

#### Shipping and the Surly Sales Representative: Part II

Sitting in her office on Friday afternoon, Chris thought long and hard about whether she really wanted to get involved in a political battle with Charlie. To make her decision, she answered the five questions discussed below.

1. Am I getting what I want? "It's not working at all. Charlie hasn't budged and our shipping errors seem to be increasing."
2. What are my interests and are they at stake? "Unless I can get this problem addressed, I may not even have a job in three months. Clearly, my interests are at stake."
3. How likely is it that I can succeed in getting what I need? "I don't have a lot of leverage with Charlie because he's such a top performer, even though many people think he's a pain to work with. However, Charlie's boss, Deanna, is usually very reasonable. I may not get everything I need, but I suspect she can help move us in the right direction."
4. How good are my working relationships with the people involved? "It's clear that my relationship with Charlie and probably Eric could use some work. They both like to play unconstructive political games. But my relationship with Deanna is positive and my own staff is very supportive."
5. What is the priority of this particular battle? "It's critical to our mission." ■

After answering these questions, Chris went right to work thinking about her strategy. Monday morning would come fast and this was a battle she had to fight.

## Exercise 2.2

Identify the most pressing political challenge with which you are presently faced. Describe and evaluate this political situation by filling in the chart below, and briefly answer the questions that follow the chart. (NOTE: The challenge you identify here will be drawn upon throughout the remainder of this book, so take extra care when completing this exercise and make sure the challenge is one that is important to you.)

### Political Challenge: What are the major issues involved in this situation?

Who are the other key players; what are their needs, interests, concerns; how much power and influence do they have in this situation; and how good is your working relationship with each person?

| Player | Interests, Needs, or Concerns | Power and Influence | Working Relationship |
|---|---|---|---|
| YOU | | | |
| | | | |
| | | | |
| | | | |
| | | | |

What have you done so far to influence this situation? Is it working?

What are your interests in this situation? What do you need here to be satisfied and fulfilled?

What are your chances of being successful in getting what you need in this situation?

How could you get what you need without getting into this battle? What might you gain? What might you lose?

# Chapter Checkpoints

✓ Political activity often centers around the following decisions:

- Who gets to participate in what.
- Who gets what information.
- Who is responsible for what.
- Who gets what resources.
- Staffing.
- Who gets credit or blame.
- Coordination of related activities across people or groups.
- Major organizational changes.

✓ The common denominator in all political situations is conflict between people over things they care about.

✓ Choose your political battles wisely by asking the following five key questions:

1. Are my present actions helping me get the results I want?
2. What are my interests and are they at stake here?
3. How likely is it that I can succeed in getting what I need here?
4. How good are my working relationships with the people involved?
5. What is the priority of this particular battle?

CHAPTER

# 3 Political Strategies

**This chapter will help you to:**

- Identify the five basic political strategies.
- Identify the political strategies you have been using at work.

**Shipping and the Surly Sales Representative: Part III**

Chris saw her manager, Eric, trudging down the hall toward her office. He was staring at the floor, shoulders stooped. He looked tired and beaten.

"I just got another call from Deanna," Eric said as he sat down in Chris's office. From the expression on Eric's face, Chris knew that Deanna had called Eric to complain about something. "She's livid. We shipped another incorrect order to Megatron. That's the third shipping error to them in the past two months. They claim that their receiving department has had to spend 40 person-hours sorting out each shipment and packaging returns to us. They want us to reimburse them for the time. Even worse, they have promised Deanna that one more shipping error will cost us their account—they will find another vendor."

Eric paused and swallowed hard before continuing. "Chris, I know that Megatron is one of Charlie's accounts. I know that when Charlie receives an order from Megatron or any of his other clients, he often waits several days before sending you the paperwork. I know that he calls and leaves incomplete shipping instructions on your voicemail after work hours. I know that this makes it extremely difficult for you to service Megatron properly. And I also know that Charlie is a pain in the neck to work with. He's rude, he's uncooperative, and he's a bully. But Chris, it's your job to figure out how to work with sales reps like Charlie and to make accurate shipments to clients.

"If Megatron was the only client that was complaining about shipping problems, I probably wouldn't be too concerned. But it's not just them, Chris. Deanna mentioned several other clients who have called to grouse about shipping errors. This can't continue. I need an action plan from you for correcting this mess by 9 A.M. tomorrow." ■

## BASIC POLITICAL STRATEGIES

Although it is clear that Chris has a bigger problem than just figuring out what to do about Charlie, her conflict with him is critical to turning the situation around. Here are five possible strategies:

**Strategy 1:** Chris could avoid dealing directly with Charlie to solve the problem. Although he is a big contributor to the shipping mess, she could find ways to avoid or delay a potentially explosive confrontation. She could, for example, distract everyone by proposing a broad, time-consuming study of the work flow between Sales and Shipping. Or she could call the company's Total Quality Group and suggest that the time was ripe for them to propose quality training for her department. Either way, her strategy would be to avoid dealing directly with the conflict by drawing attention away from her problem with Charlie.



**Strategy 2:** Chris could propose that her department find ways to deal more effectively with Charlie's "organic" (i.e., confusing and unreliable) approach to calling in orders. She could communicate to her people that customer satisfaction is a primary value for the shipping department and that Charlie is one of their most important "internal" customers. She could then call Charlie and thank him for drawing her attention to the overly bureaucratic process that has developed over time in the shipping department (largely due to the personality of her predecessor, of course). She could assure him that her staff will do everything they can to treat him like their best customer.

**Strategy 3:** Chris could mount a campaign to convince everyone that Sales, in general, and Charlie, in particular, are to blame for the "customer service" problem (notice that it would no longer be called a "shipping" problem). She could call for a "crisis" meeting between Sales and Shipping, probably while Charlie is out of town. In preparation for the meeting, she could ask her staff to gather a detailed record showing how the vast majority of customer service problems have been a result of Sales' failure to follow the company's order placement procedure. At the meeting, she could even play back Charlie's most confusing voice messages and pass around his most illegible written orders.

**Strategy 4:** Chris could try to cut a special deal with Charlie—perhaps offering to give his customers priority over those of the other sales reps—if he agrees to submit his orders every day. The overall performance and responsiveness of Chris's department might suffer a bit, but at least it would solve the immediate problem with Charlie.

**Strategy 5:** Chris could call Charlie immediately and arrange to meet him at his field office. During the meeting, she could describe the problem in clear, neutral language. She could ask Charlie to describe his view of the problem. Then she

3

could explain her real needs to Charlie and ask him to explain how his present method helped him meet his own interests. She also could ask him why he cannot follow the regular order submission procedure. These questions may help clarify his underlying interests and concerns. Then she could ask him to help her brainstorm alternatives that would satisfy both their interests. If Charlie blames her or questions the competence of her department, Chris could deflect the energy of the attack right back at the problem, rather than taking it personally. She could refuse to be lured back into one of the other strategies until she has exhausted her efforts for a win-win solution.

## Exercise 3.1

What do you think of the five strategies discussed above? In the table below, identify the potential cost and benefit of each.

| | Cost | Benefit |
|---|---|---|
| Strategy 1: | ______________ | ______________ |
| Strategy 2: | ______________ | ______________ |
| Strategy 3: | ______________ | ______________ |
| Strategy 4: | ______________ | ______________ |
| Strategy 5: | ______________ | ______________ |

Considering the costs and benefits that you have identified, which strategy would you recommend to Chris? If that one did not work, which would you try next?

## COMPARING POLITICAL STRATEGIES

Each of the five strategies discussed above represents a different approach to dealing with political situations. These strategies are avoidance, accommodation, competition, compromise, and collaboration.*

---

*They were originally proposed by Kenneth Thomas: *see* Kenneth Thomas, *Conflict and Negotiation Processes,* in *Handbook of Industrial Organizational Psychology,* vol. 3, 2nd ed., ed. Marvin Dunnette and Leaetta Hough (Palo Alto, Calif.: Consulting Psychologists Press, 1992).

Your actions in any political situation are based on your goals with respect to (*a*) satisfying your own needs or interests and (*b*) satisfying the needs and interests of the other player(s).

Your political strategy is based on where you stand on these two goals. For example, if you decide that your goal is to pursue your own interests without regard for the other person's interests, your strategy will be to compete in a win-lose fashion. If your goal is to pursue your own interests *and* the other person's interests, your strategy will be to collaborate—a win-win approach.



The following table illustrates for the five political strategies whether or not you seek to satisfy your own interests or the other player's interests.

| Strategy | Do You Seek to Satisfy Your Own Interests? | Do You Seek to Satisfy the Other Player's Interests? |
|---|---|---|
| Avoidance | No | No |
| Accommodation | No | Yes |
| Competition | Yes | No |
| Compromise | Yes and No | Yes and No |
| Collaboration | Yes | Yes |

Let's take a closer look at the five political strategies.

# AVOIDANCE

One of Chris's options is to avoid dealing with her conflict with Charlie. In using this avoidance strategy, she chooses to ignore Charlie's interests and most of her own interests. She does manage to avoid losing in a direct confrontation with Charlie—for now. But her other interests, such as satisfying customers and meeting her department's performance objectives, are neglected.

Chris can pursue the avoidance strategy in a variety of ways. One is to bury her head in the sand like an ostrich, hoping the storm will blow over or that people will forget about the shipping errors. A more active way is to distract people away from the problem. Chris could use a more active approach (as illustrated in Strategy 1) by calling for a broad-based work flow study or total quality training.

Some of the pitfalls of the avoidance strategy include:

- In the long run, the avoidance strategy is not personally satisfying if you care about making a positive contribution. Your opinions and suggestions are ignored. You feel little pride in your work. And worst of all, you know that you are avoiding tough situations that need handling. Nothing can damage your self-esteem as much as living with the awareness that you are the kind of person who cannot deal with difficult problems.

- The avoidance strategy is career limiting in an organization that values performance. Such organizations typically promote people who get results. Having good ideas is not enough; you must be able to make things happen.

- When the avoidance strategy becomes a way of life in an organization, the organization quickly loses its vitality and adaptability. It begins to die. Resources are used to avoid blame rather than to produce great products or services. Avoidance is almost always a short-sighted solution.



## Exercise 3.2

Recall a time when you or someone you know used the avoidance strategy when faced with a difficult political situation. What was the situation? What did you or the person you know do? How did the other party to the dispute respond? What were the consequences for the problem and for the relationship with the other party?

______________________________________________

______________________________________________

______________________________________________

______________________________________________

______________________________________________

______________________________________________

3

# ACCOMMODATION

The second option open to Chris is to focus on satisfying Charlie's interests—at the expense of her own as illustrated in Strategy 2 above. Since Charlie is one of her "internal" customers, she can take the "customer is always right" stance and bend over backward to make sure he is happy. She can apologize for upsetting him, smooth over any conflict with him, and attempt to become his friend. Her hope is that her efforts will cause Charlie to be more cooperative and considerate in the future.

The disadvantages of the accommodation strategy are as follows:

- The accommodation strategy does not solve the problem. Without Charlie's cooperation, the best Chris can do is to come up with a Band-Aid fix for the shipping errors. This is a cross-department problem that requires adjustment on both sides. While Chris is spending her time trying to become Charlie's friend, the company's performance will continue to suffer.
- The accommodation strategy does not build positive political relationships. Even if Chris gives in to Charlie on the shipping problem, there is no guarantee that Charlie will cooperate with Chris in the future. In fact, one of the best ways to bring out the bully in others is to reward them for bullying. You cannot buy a relationship by giving in to someone's demands. You can only earn a relationship through mutual problem solving and respect.

## Exercise 3.3

Recall a time when you or someone you know accommodated the other party in a political dispute rather than face the difficult political situation head-on? What was the situation? What did you or the person you know do to accommodate the other party? What were the results of this strategy? What is the quality of the relationship with the other party now?

## COMPETITION

Chris's third option is to attack Charlie like a shark, taking bites out of him until he agrees to negotiate with her. This strategy is based on the assumption that this is a win-lose, survival-of-the-fittest dispute. Like a shark, Chris can choose to attack just once or hit him again and again. Strategy 3 above illustrates just a few of the ways Chris can work for her own interests by undermining Charlie's. If Chris's attacks are successful, Charlie will be forced to cooperate with her, and others will think twice about crossing her again. On the other hand, Charlie appears to be a very powerful shark himself. He may prove strong enough to counterattack and devour Chris!

People who adopt the competition strategy often enjoy short-term success. But their long-term career prospects are poor because allies come and go, but enemies accumulate.



## Exercise 3.4

Recall a time when you or someone you know used the competition strategy, showing little or no concern for the interests or needs of others. What was the situation? What did you or the person you know do? How did the other party respond? Did you or the person you know achieve the desired short-term goals? How did using the strategy affect the relationship with the other party? In the long term, was this strategy effective?

# COMPROMISE

A fourth option for Chris is to haggle and bargain with Charlie. She may not get everything she wants, but neither will Charlie. At least they will be able to keep moving ahead rather than remaining gridlocked. As a shipping supervisor, Chris is in a position to do favors for Charlie and his customers. She can offer him a deal (see Strategy 4). For example, she can give his most important customer top priority—she will ship this customer's goods as soon as she receives the order, even if there are other orders pending—provided Charlie submits all his orders every day. Charlie may not agree right away. He may insist that Chris give priority to his 5 or 10 most important customers, but Chris is confident they will be able to piece together a deal.

The compromise strategy can take you part of the way toward playing positive politics. Habitual compromisers, however, often get caught up in their bartering, trading, and scheming. They make promises they cannot keep and forget to keep the promises that they have made. They are rarely satisfied with an agreement. Inevitably, they try to reopen negotiations, looking for a more favorable settlement for themselves. This creates mistrust and destroys long-term relationships. Others begin to anticipate the compromiser's cunning and trickery, and often they respond in kind. Both parties quickly fall back to the competition strategy, in which one party wins and the other party loses.

### Exercise 3.5

Recall a time when you or someone you know bartered, haggled, and schemed to obtain a favorable solution to a political problem. What was the situation? How did you or the person you know compromise? How did you or the person you know feel about the agreement? How did the other party feel?

## COLLABORATION: THE STRATEGY OF CHOICE

Chris may decide that her best course of action is to seek a solution that will meet Charlie's interests and hers (see Strategy 5 above). She will invite Charlie to talk about what he needs and work together to brainstorm options. When attacked, she will not hesitate to defend her real needs and interests—she will be consistently assertive. And she will do everything she can to keep her cool and not give in to the temptation to switch prematurely to a competition, accommodation, avoidance, or compromise strategy. Her goal will be to work with Charlie until they reach an agreement that is fully acceptable to both of them.

The collaboration strategy can be used to solve political problems constructively. If you are truly interested in getting results and building relationships, the collaboration strategy is the strategy of choice. If Chris uses this strategy to deal with Charlie, she can expect several positive outcomes:

- Chris can use her power to move Charlie toward a solution that meets his needs and hers.
- Chris can build a long-term relationship with Charlie by showing that she is willing to work with him on problems that matter to both of them.
- By collaborating, Chris increases the value of her stock as a future leader in her organization. Organizations invest heavily in the training, development, and career advancement of employees who get results and have a reputation of being a good person to work with.
- Chris will feel good about herself for taking a positive, effective approach to resolving her conflict with Charlie. Her self-esteem will be enhanced.

## Exercise 3.6

Recall a time when you or someone you know used the collaboration strategy to deal with a workplace conflict. What was the conflict? What did you or the person you know do? How did the other party respond? How were your or the other person's work, the relationship with the other party, and self-esteem affected?

______________________________

______________________________

______________________________

______________________________

______________________________

______________________________

## Exercise 3.7

This exercise will help you to identify which one of the five political strategies you are pursuing in the political challenge you described in Exercise 2.2 on page 17. Complete the quiz below by placing a check mark in either the "Agree" or "Disagree" column for each statement, and then total your scores.

### POLITICAL STRATEGY QUIZ

#### Part 1

| | Agree | Disagree |
|---|---|---|
| **1.** I have asked my "political partner" to tell me about his or her concerns and needs. | ______ | ______ |
| **2.** I have never blamed my political partner for causing our problem, nor have I become defensive when my political partner has blamed me. | ______ | ______ |
| **3.** I have told my political partner that his or her concerns are valid and important to me. | ______ | ______ |
| **4.** I have told my political partner that I want to have a positive work relationship with him or her. | ______ | ______ |
| **5.** I am looking for a solution that will address my political partner's needs and concerns. | ______ | ______ |
| **6.** I have never used more force or power than necessary to persuade my partner to negotiate with me. | ______ | ______ |
| Total number of check marks in the "Agree" column: | ______________ | |

#### Part 2

| | Agree | Disagree |
|---|---|---|
| **1.** I have discussed my needs and concerns with my political partner. | ______ | ______ |
| **2.** I have not tried to "keep the peace" or build a long-term relationship with my political partner by giving in to demands that will conflict with my own needs. | ______ | ______ |
| **3.** I have tried to convince my political partner that he or she needs to help find ways of satisfying my needs in this situation. | ______ | ______ |
| **4.** I have suggested solutions to the problem that will satisfy my needs. | ______ | ______ |

| | Agree | Disagree |
|---|---|---|
| **5.** I am looking for a solution that will fully address my needs and concerns. | ______ | ______ |
| **6.** If necessary, I will use force or power to persuade my partner to negotiate with me. | ______ | ______ |
| Total number of check marks in the "Agree" column: | ____________ | |



To determine the strategy you used, find your scores for both Parts 1 and 2 in the table below. Your score on Part 1 reflects your desire to satisfy your adversary's interests. Your score on Part 2 reflects your desire to satisfy your own interests. Your strategy can be found next to the row that contains both your scores.

| | Number of Agree Checks | |
|---|---|---|
| **Strategy Used** | **Score on Part 1** | **Score on Part 2** |
| Avoidance | 1–2 | 1–2 |
| Accommodation | 5–6 | 1–2 |
| Competition | 1–2 | 5–6 |
| Compromise | 3–4 | 3–4 |
| Collaboration | 5–6 | 5–6 |

If you are using the collaboration strategy in your political situation, congratulations! You are on the road to political success. If you are not using the collaboration strategy, think about why you are not:

- Is the situation unimportant to you? Do you have little interest in gaining a favorable solution?
- Is the relationship unimportant to you? Do you think you will never have to see or work with this person again? Can you be sure of that? If this is someone you will have to work with in the future, you will need a positive relationship—even if you do not like the person.

# Chapter Checkpoints

✓ The five most common political strategies are avoidance, accommodation, competition, compromise, and collaboration.

✓ Collaboration is the only positive political strategy.

✓ Although you may have a "typical" political strategy, you probably use different strategies in different situations.

✓ You *can* learn to use the collaboration strategy to deal with your most significant political challenges.

CHAPTER

# 4 Getting Results

**This chapter will help you to:**

- Distinguish issues, solutions, and interests.
- Protect yourself with a political insurance policy.
- Brainstorm creative, collaborative solutions.
- Search with your partner for benchmarks to help create fair solutions.

In this chapter, you will learn to use collaboration to get the results you care about. The following principles are the political equivalent of blocking and tackling in football. Learn and practice these principles and your political effectiveness will grow exponentially. These are the keys to collaboration:

1. Identify issues, solutions, and interests.
2. Take out a political insurance policy.
3. Brainstorm collaborative solutions.
4. Look for benchmarks.

## IDENTIFY ISSUES, SOLUTIONS, AND INTERESTS

Political conflicts become deadlocked almost immediately when the parties start taking hard stands on the issues. Think back on the story of Chris and Charlie (in Chapter 2). Charlie's behavior—stonewalling Chris and refusing to change—sends a very clear message to Chris. He is not going to change; she will have to change to accommodate him. Chris's actions also communicate the solution she wants: Charlie must follow the procedure like everyone else. Even though Chris and Charlie want some of the same things—customer satisfaction and efficient order handling—their proposed solutions ignore their common interest and set the stage for a competitive battle. The more they publicly commit themselves to their own solutions, the more they dig in and turn the situation into a win–lose power struggle.

To negotiate political conflict, you must first understand the distinction between issues, solutions, and interests.



**Issues** are the *questions* you must answer in order to reach a satisfying agreement. Common political issues may include:

- What will be the roles and responsibilities of this new job?
- How many new employees will be added to our department this year?
- When will the design specification for the new product be delivered?
- What will the new commission percentage be?

**Solutions** are *possible answers* to the questions raised by issues. Possible solutions to the issues mentioned above are:

- The new job will include responsibility for implementing sales promotions to distributors.
- We will add four new employees to the department.
- The design specifications will be delivered on June 30.
- Commissions next year will be 11 percent of sales.

**Interests** are the *underlying needs,* goals, hopes, fears, and concerns that you want to achieve or avoid in the political situation. Examples include:

- Increasing control over key department activies.
- Increasing the department's ability to respond quickly to customers.
- Gaining additional time to work out bugs in the current design specifications.
- Increasing sales revenues to avoid loss of employment.

It is important to identify the issues and underlying interests involved in order to negotiate successfully for yourself. It is also important to recognize that a number of different solutions may satisfy your interests. Your goal in political situations should be to satisfy your underlying interests, not to make sure your solution is the one chosen.

1. **Think through and write out your own interests *before* you meet with the other parties involved.** Time spent in such preparation is one of the wisest investments you can make.
2. **Do not guess about what your partner really needs and wants.** If your partner has not identified his or her interests or will not tell you directly what they are, you will have to investigate. Here are some good ways to do it:
   - Look for clues about your partner's interests in his or her proposed solution. If you go along with the proposal, what will your partner gain? What will he or she lose? Even more important, what does your partner think he or she will gain or lose?
   - Ask your partner, "Why do you think we should do that?" This question invites your partner to talk about his or her underlying interests. The more you know about what your partner thinks he or she needs, the more likely you are to come up with a solution that satisfies you both.
   - Ask your partner, "What if we do this [some other course of action] instead? When you propose a solution and ask, "What if . . . ?" most people cannot resist giving you their opinion. Their opinion will give you lots of information about their underlying interests that they otherwise might not share directly with you.
3. **When another person in the conflict proposes a solution, respond with, "That's a possibility."** You do not need to reject a proposed solution; you need to reposition it as one possible way of handling the situation—a way that may or may not help everyone realize their interests.
4. **Make a written list of each person's interests, and let the others know what you are doing.** For example, you might say, "I want to make sure I understand each of our goals, needs, and concerns here so we can find a good solution for everyone." You may want to write them on a white board or flip chart where everyone can see them.
5. **Listen openly to other persons' opinions, beliefs, interests, and proposed solutions in order to understand their points of view.** You do not have to agree with them to understand them. But you cannot collaborate unless you understand.

## Exercise 4.1

Recall the political challenge you identified in Exercise 2.2 (page 17), and answer the following questions.

1. What are the key issues that you and your partner need to address in this situation?

   ______________________________________________

   ______________________________________________

2. What solutions have been proposed so far?

   ______________________________________________

   ______________________________________________

3. What have you done so far to communicate your interests to your partner?

   ______________________________________________

   ______________________________________________

4. What could you do immediately or in your next meeting to get everyone focused on the key issues?

   ______________________________________________

   ______________________________________________

## TAKE OUT A POLITICAL INSURANCE POLICY

To execute the collaboration strategy successfully, you must sincerely believe that you and your partner can create a satisfying solution.

But sometimes even your best efforts will fail to produce an agreement. You will need a backup solution that will allow you to continue to pursue your interests and needs without any help from the other person. In political conflicts, it is helpful to think of your backup solution as your "political insurance policy."

A good political insurance policy increases your comfort and confidence. If you know that you have another way of getting what you need without the coöperation of your partner, you will be less inclined to accept an agreement that shortchanges your interests.

A good political insurance policy also increases your power. It protects you against crippling loss, should you need to walk away. This makes you less susceptible to pressure tactics from the other person. You can stand your ground and keep insisting on a fair, collaborative solution.

It is crucial to remember, however, that the person you are working with also has an insurance policy, even if he or she has not thought specifically about it. If this person's policy protects his or her interests better than your policy protects yours, you will be at a disadvantage.



To create an effective political insurance policy:

**1. Review what is covered in your insurance policy.** Before you meet with the other person or group to work on a problem, invest some time in asking yourself, "What will I do if I cannot reach an agreement that satisfies my interests?"

Study your policy carefully! It is easy to fool yourself into thinking you are covered when you are not. You may think, "Well, if this doesn't work out, I could take a job in another division, switch companies, or even change careers." But what specifically would you do? Do you have any assurance that one of these possibilities is a sure option for you?

Applying this step to Chris and Charlie's situation, Chris needs to think about what she will do if Charlie continues to stonewall her or proposes an unsatisfactory compromise. Is there a way for her to get the results she wants without getting an agreement from Charlie? How dependent is she on him for achieving her interests and satisfying her needs?

**2. Upgrade your insurance policy.** Once you have reviewed your policy, you may find that it is time to buy more coverage—that is, to increase the range of alternate options. For example, if Chris's current insurance policy is simply to pass the problem along to Juan, her assistant, she probably should consider upgrading her policy. She does not have enough protection. One way to do so would be to convince Eric, her manager, to back her up in her confrontation with Charlie. With his support, she has more protection against a crippling loss in her dealings with Charlie.

**3. Investigate your partner's insurance policy.** What will your partner do if there is no agreement? Does your partner think he will be able to satisfy his interests without working with you? Answering these questions will give you a direct reading on how much power your partner has over you in this situation. If you think your partner's insurance policy is unlikely to satisfy his needs as well as you can, it is often helpful to ask him directly, "If we can't agree to work together on this, what will you do? How will that help you satisfy your interests?" Do not tell your partner what will happen; ask questions that will allow him to discover on his own that his own policy is not very good and that he needs your help to satisfy his interests.



If Chris were to think about Charlie's insurance policy, she might conclude that Charlie thinks he can get his way by applying political pressure through his manager, Deanna. Given his reputation and connections, Charlie probably will be able to pull this off. But he may be underestimating the amount of time and energy it will take to make this happen. If Charlie continues to stonewall her, Chris may want to ask him to think through the negative consequences (e.g., time and energy wasted) of escalating their disagreement to management.

**4. Use your insurance policy only when you need it.** When do you tell your political partner about your insurance policy? If you have a very good one that covers most of your interests, it is tempting to tell your partner right away in hopes of motivating him or her to reach an agreement quickly. The danger is that the perception will be that you are using your insurance policy as a threat. Generally speaking, you should tell your partner about your insurance policy as a last resort *after* you have done all you can within the time available to reach an agreement. Although talking about your policy may be necessary for motivating your partner to work collaboratively, using your policy means that you have given up on working with the person. This puts your working relationship at risk.

## Exercise 4.2

Recall the political challenge you identified in Exercise 2.2 (page 17), and answer the following questions.

1. What is your insurance policy in this situation? Which of your interests does it cover?

   ________________________________________

   ________________________________________

2. What can you do to upgrade your insurance policy?

   ________________________________________

   ________________________________________

3. What is your political partner's insurance policy? Will it meet his or her needs? Has your partner thought through the consequences of using it?

______________________________________________

______________________________________________

4. When should you tell your partner about your insurance policy? How do you think your partner will respond?

______________________________________________

______________________________________________



## BRAINSTORM COLLABORATIVE SOLUTIONS

The next step is to expand the number of solutions you have to choose from. Too often, you fail to take even a moment to think creatively about what might be possible. When a political conflict escalates, tension rises, defensiveness takes hold, and your ability and willingness to entertain new ideas contracts even more.

Think about Chris and Charlie. What solutions have they entertained so far? Pretty limited, aren't they? And notice that their solutions are one-sided—they satisfy one person's interests but not the other's. Chris and Charlie need to generate more solutions—collaborative solutions—that will satisfy them both.

Brainstorming is one of the best ways to create collaborative solutions. Although most people know how brainstorming works, it takes discipline to make it work. The following guidelines are crucial to successful brainstorming:

1. **Set aside a time for brainstorming.** Unless you schedule a time for brainstorming, you might not ever take the time needed to identify creative potential solutions to your problem.
2. **Criticism of solutions is *not allowed* during brainstorming.** Criticism completely shuts down creativity.
3. **If at all possible, brainstorm *with* your political adversaries.** When the rules are followed, brainstorming is a powerful way of getting people to stop competing and begin working together. And when the best solutions are selected for further consideration at the end of brainstorming, there is a stronger sense that they are jointly, rather than individually, owned.

**4. Try to create solutions that satisfy both parties.** If you and your partners are having difficulty developing solutions that meet everyone's interests, suggest that each person step out of his or her own role and into yours or someone else's. Then ask, "What solutions might you suggest if you were [that person]?"

**5. Select the "best solutions"—those that satisfy the interests of all the parties involved—for further consideration.**



### Exercise 4.3

Recall the political challenge you identified in Exercise 2.2 (page 17), and answer the following questions.

1. What solutions have you and your partner considered so far?

______________________________

______________________________

2. To what extent do these solutions satisfy the interests of all the parties involved?

______________________________

______________________________

3. What could you do immediately or at your next meeting to expand and enrich the available solutions? What are the obstacles to brainstorming in this situation?

______________________________

______________________________

## LOOK FOR BENCHMARKS

Sometimes in political situations even your best efforts to come up with a collaborative solution fall short. In Chris and Charlie's case, for example, Charlie may have an underlying interest in simply being able to do his job exactly the way he wants to do it. This interest in complete freedom is in direct conflict with Chris's need to ensure that orders are processed in the most efficient and timely manner. Charlie's autonomy in this case is purchased at Chris's expense.

Fortunately, there is a way to play positive politics when interests collide. The answer is to search for a solution to a *benchmark* that both players accept as fair and reasonable. A benchmark is consistent with positive politics because it gets the best results possible while maintaining conditions for a healthy working relationship.

Here are examples of benchmarks that can help resolve conflicting interests in a positive way:

- Best practices in your industry.
- Precedents from similar situations in your organization.
- Opinions of people you both regard as experts.
- Data from jointly conducted studies or surveys.



If she is to play positive politics with Charlie, Chris probably will need to bring benchmarks into play. Charlie has turned the situation into a contest of wills and seems pretty confident of winning. Furthermore, he seems to have more influence than Chris and is likely to use it in a power struggle. Chris needs to change the rules of the game.

To use benchmarks most effectively in her conflict with Charlie, Chris needs to meet Charlie in person. When Charlie insists that he will continue to submit orders his way, Chris can say:

"OK, Charlie, that's one possible solution to our problem. I recognize that you need a lot of freedom to do your job and that you don't want to get all hung up in administrative detail. But I've got a job to do too, and I can't be successful without some help from you on this problem. Rather than wasting a lot more of our time battling each other on this one, what if we look together for a fair and objective way of resolving this disagreement? For example, we could do a conference call to Mark Rosenshein in Sales over at MC Industries. I've heard you talk before about the outstanding quality program that Mark has implemented, and we both know that MC has a great reputation for quality. I'm sure Mark has dealt with this problem before and can help us. Can we both agree to try to implement whatever solutions Mark recommends? Or do you have other ideas about where we could get an objective, independent opinion on this issue?"

A key to using benchmarks successfully is to agree up front to **look for the benchmarks together, not separately.** If you look separately, the benchmarks you come up with will be suspect to your partner. For example, your partner might believe that you picked a particular "expert" because you knew this expert would agree with you. If you look for the benchmarks together and discuss their objectivity as you do so, both of you can buy into the fairness of the resulting solution.

## Exercise 4.4

Recall the political challenge you identified in Exercise 2.2 (page 17), and answer the following questions.

1. Do any of your interests directly conflict with those of another player in the situation? Which interests?

   ______________________________

   ______________________________

2. Has either of you proposed a benchmark for resolving this conflict? What benchmarks might be relevant here? Would your partner think they were relevant? Fair? Objective?

   ______________________________

   ______________________________

3. What could you do immediately or in your next meeting to get your partner involved in looking for benchmarks?

   ______________________________

   ______________________________

# Chapter Checkpoints

✓ Sort out issues, solutions, and interests to clarify your understanding of any political situation.

✓ Do not reject your partner's solutions.

✓ Review your political insurance policy to make sure you have that coverage you need.

✓ Take time to brainstorm.

✓ When interests are in direct conflict, press your partner to look with you for independent benchmarks that you can both accept.

CHAPTER

# 5 Building Relationships

**This chapter will help you to:**

- Assert yourself with your partner.
- Keep communication channels clear and open.
- Realize the power of letting others choose for themselves.
- Build and maintain trust.

## SURFACE VERSUS SUBTERRANEAN POLITICS

On the surface, political conflicts are concerned primarily with disagreements or misunderstandings about substantive issues, such as budgets, schedules, and promotions. But if you look into these conflicts at a deeper "subterranean" level, you often discover friction in the working relationships of the people involved.

To play positive politics, you must devote at least as much attention to people and relationships as to the substance of any conflict. When working relationships break down, even the simplest substantive or technical issue can become a major drain on your personal resources and those of your organization.



To build and maintain good working relationships:

1. Assert yourself.
2. Use your head *and* your heart.
3. Understand and respect your partner.
4. Communicate directly and proactively.
5. Empower your partner to choose.
6. Invest in your relationship "trust fund."

Let's examine each principle more specifically and see how each can be useful to Chris in building her relationship with Charlie.

## ASSERT YOURSELF

Positive politics begins with assertiveness. To stand up for your interests, you must be:

- Clear about what you need to be successful and happy over the long term.
- Determined and relentless in your pursuit of the things that will make you successful and happy.
- Honest with yourself and others about what you really need and why.

Asserting yourself is not the same as being selfish or "looking out for number one." It does not mean that you insist on getting your way in every petty disagreement. You must distinguish your "big picture" needs—those things that are central to your long-term success and happiness—from your immediate desires, those things that you want right now. There may be times when it is wise for you to sacrifice your immediate desires for the good of others (e.g., when your desires are in direct conflict with the needs of a co-worker, a customer, your team, or your organization). Ask yourself, "Looking back on this three months from now, what will I wish I had done today?" Pursuing selfish desires at the expense of others is a sure way to make enemies who will be waiting for the first opportunity to turn the tables and gain their revenge.

You should make every effort to satisfy your big picture needs and interests. You must state clearly what you need (from yourself and from others) and act in ways that are consistent with your needs. You will earn the respect of others and enhance your chances of success.



Note that the avoidance and accommodation strategies fail to follow the "assert yourself" principle. Although these strategies are useful at times, consistent use of them produces a number of negative consequences, including dissatisfying results, poor working relationships, and, worst of all, low self-esteem. Applying this principle to Chris and Charlie, you can see that Chris needs to be very clear—with all the players involved—about what she needs from Charlie and the sales department to be successful in her job.

## Exercise 5.1

Recall the political challenge you identified in Exercise 2.2 (page 17), and answer the following questions.

1. What have you done to communicate your needs and interests to your partner in this political conflict? Does your partner clearly understand what you need from him or her?

   ________________________________________

   ________________________________________

2. Have you at any time in this situation backed away from asserting your interests and needs? If you have, what prompted you to do so? What were the consequences?

   ________________________________________

   ________________________________________

3. What do you need to do immediately to ensure that you stay focused on pursuing your big-picture needs and interests in this situation?

_______________________________________________

_______________________________________________



## USE YOUR HEAD *AND* YOUR HEART

Positive politics requires both rational thinking and passion. Too little or too much of either sends political conflicts spinning off in unconstructive directions.

The "let's not get emotional" game is often a balancing response to an overly emotional partner or to a fear that your own emotions may get out of control. But androidlike logic is one of the best ways to make an excitable partner even more angry, anxious, or frustrated. Avoiding passion entirely also may hide energy that you can use to generate the sense of urgency needed to solve tough problems.

Allowing yourself to be swamped by your emotions during a political conflict, however, is also a fatal error. It is virtually impossible to think clearly about substantive issues when you are trembling with anger or gritting your teeth in frustration. Pay particular attention to how you are reacting physically to the situation. What is your stomach saying? The muscles in your face? Your back? When your body signals high emotion, it is time to step back to recover your emotional balance. Take a five-minute recess, take a short walk, or take a deep breath and count to ten.

Have you ever noticed that two people talking together often mirror each other's body language; for example, crossing their arms, leaning against a wall? This is a very natural human social response that you can use effectively in political conflicts. If you display warmth, compassion, excitement, and reason, your partner is likely to return the favor. But if you act cool and indifferent to your partner, he or she probably will act the same way toward you.

It may be difficult for Chris to keep her head and her heart enaged at the same time while dealing with Charlie. He has a reputation as a bully, and one of his favorite tactics is to throw people off balance emotionally to get them to forget temporarily about all their interests. When meeting with Charlie, Chris must keep focused on what her interests are and be able to monitor signals from her head and her heart, being prepared to take a time-out if necessary to regain her balance between the two.

## Exercise 5.2

Recall the political challenge you identified in Exercise 2.2 (page 17), and answer the following questions.

1. Have there been times when you have lost your reason or your emotion in working with the people involved in this situation? What prompted this loss of balance? What did you say or do? How did they respond?

   ______________________________

   ______________________________

2. Have there been times when your partner in this situation lost his or her balance in working with you? What do you think knocked your partner off balance? How did your behavior affect his or her balance?

   ______________________________

   ______________________________

3. What can you do to keep your head and your heart engaged in this situation? What can you do to help your partner keep his or hers engaged?

   ______________________________

   ______________________________



# UNDERSTAND AND RESPECT YOUR PARTNER

The two most critical skills needed to become a positive politician are understanding and respecting your partner.

**Understand your partner's interests, needs, hopes, and fears.** Unless you understand what the other person cares about or is afraid of, there is virtually no way to get great results or to build a long-term working relationship.

The key to understanding your partner is active listening. Becoming a good listener will enable you to achieve better results and more efficient, effective, enjoyable working relationships.

**Respect your partner's value as a human being and his or her right to personal interests, feelings, and opinions.** When you do not accept people (or their interests) as valuable and worthy of your respect, they can feel it in their bones. A lack of respect is often communicated in very subtle ways—for example, by deep sighs, a look of disbelief, or impatient finger tapping. Or it may be communicated in a more obvious manner—for example, by stereotyping, blaming, or acting condescendingly.

When you communicate a lack of respect, your behavior usually sets off a chain reaction in your political partners. Your lack of acceptance triggers their doubts and insecurities, which in turn shoots holes in their self-esteem, causing them to be defensive. They may fight you, attack you, ignore you, or run away from you—but they almost certainly will not negotiate rationally with you.



How can you do a better job of understanding and respecting your partner?

- Ask open-ended questions that begin with "what," "how," "who," "when," or "why." (But be careful not to sound like a trial lawyer conducting an interrogation!) Give the person an invitation to say what he or she is thinking rather than just responding to what you are thinking. Avoid "leading the witness" with closed-ended questions that can be answered with a "yes" or "no." These questions typically begin with words like "do," "are," "could," or "will."
- Be quiet and give your partner time to talk.
- Avoid stereotyping your partner. When you stereotype people, you assume that they have particular needs because they happen to be, for example, a male, an engineer, an extrovert, or a single parent. Not all males, engineers, extroverts, or single parents are alike; their needs differ. Treat your partner as a unique individual, and take the time to understand his or her unique needs.
- Wait until you fully understand what your partner is saying before you express your own opinion.
- Recognize that you do not have to agree with your partner's opinions or behavior in order to respect him or her as a valuable human being.
- When you disagree with what your partner says or does, focus on the behavior, not on the person.

In Chris and Charlie's case, if Chris is to influence Charlie in order to get what she needs, she will have to understand his interests and respect him as a person, perhaps even more than he will have to understand and respect her. Otherwise, Chris will continue to run head-on into Charlie's defenses and waste time on proposals and requests that he resists.

### Exercise 5.3

Recall the political challenge you identified in Exercise 2.2 (page 17), and answer the following questions.

1. How well do you understand what it looks like and feels like to be your partner in this situation?

   ______________________________________________

   ______________________________________________

2. What have you done to communicate to your partner that you care about and value him or her as a person? What have you done that may have led your partner to feel rejected?

   ______________________________________________

   ______________________________________________

3. What do you need to do differently to communicate your acceptance and to develop your understanding?

   ______________________________________________

   ______________________________________________



## COMMUNICATE DIRECTLY AND PROACTIVELY

"We have a communication problem!" Communication seems to be at the root of much organizational confusion and conflict. Because people and situations change constantly, we depend on close communication with others to adjust our priorities and to stay in synch with the organization's changing strategies and tactics.

Entire books have been written on principles of communication. Here are the critical principles to know when dealing with political situations:

**1. Whenever possible, "label" your behavior for your political partners *before* you act.** For example, if you are going to talk to your boss about a problem with one of your political partners, tell your partner before you do so and explain why. If you are not going to call your partner for three days, tell him or her so and explain why. Some of the greatest political mischief has been caused by misinterpretations of people's behavior. When you do not label your behavior for others, any insecurities they have about you or your relationship rise to the surface. The result is usually a defensive interpretation (e.g., "He doesn't care what I think," "She's trying to work around me," etc.).

**2. When you have a problem with someone, talk directly to him or her about it, no matter how anxious or fearful you feel about doing so.** Communication triangles in which John speaks to Pedro about his problem with Sharon are deadly for all the work relationships involved.

**3. Respect the interests and needs of an absent partner.** If at all possible, avoid making decisions that will have a dramatic impact on individuals who are unable to attend a decision meeting. If this is not feasible, you should take into account the interests of the missing person.



**4. When tensions rise and conflicts escalate, communicate more rather than less.** Our natural instinct is to move away from people who are making us uncomfortable. But, to flee simply makes the problems worse and denies you the chance to work through them.

**5. Communicate messages with strong emotional content face-to-face whenever possible.** Phone calls, letters, voicemail, electronic mail, and messengers almost always distort the message you want to send. These media do not include the most important channel for communicating emotional messages—nonverbal behavior, or body language.

In Chris's situation with Charlie, she has made some communication mistakes that she needs to correct. First, she needs to communicate more often with Charlie and she needs to meet with him face-to-face. This will give her a better chance to understand Charlie's concerns, communicate her own needs, and clearly describe how she feels about the situation. She must avoid working through intermediaries such as Eric. And she should consult with Charlie before taking any action that will affect his interests.

## Exercise 5.4

Recall the political situation you identified in Exercise 2.2 (page 17), and answer the following questions.

1. How would you describe the communication channels among the key players in your political situation? What is working? What is not working?

___

___

2. What can you do right away to improve communication in this situation?

______________________________________________

______________________________________________

## EMPOWER YOUR PARTNER TO CHOOSE

Few political tactics are as damaging to working relationships as forcing your partner to do things your way. Even when you are trying to impose a solution that is "for [his or her] own good," it is likely that you will damage the relationship permanently and make your future dealings with your partner more difficult. Your partner probably will find it difficult, if not impossible, to accept the forced agreement and is likely to look for opportunities to undermine or sabotage it. The negative long-term consequences of reducing others' freedom to choose rarely justify the short-term, illusory benefits.



One of the best ways to recognize your own "forcing" tactics is to ask yourself how you would feel if someone forced an agreement on you. How do you feel when someone does any of the following?

- Acts like he or she knows all the answers and that you would understand if you were smarter.
- Tells you to "take it or leave it."
- Avoids or stonewalls you.
- Threatens to take the problem over your head or otherwise make trouble for you.
- Is willing to discuss only one or two possible solutions to the problem.
- Goes behind your back to lobby his or her own support from others.

When these tactics are used on us, we directly feel the damage they do. But we sometimes fail to see that we use these tactics ourselves, with equally damaging consequences for our working relationships.

Instead of using "forcing" tactics, you can use the "power of the problem" to help your partner see the likely consequences of his or her proposed solutions. For example, if your partner threatens to escalate a disagreement to your boss, ask him or her to think through the consequences with you. Ask the following questions:

- What do you think the boss will decide?
- How do you think the boss will feel about having to deal with this issue?
- How will going to the boss affect his or her perception of our ability to work together? Of our problem-solving skills?
- Are there other more difficult issues we may need the boss's help with later?
- How do you think having to go to the boss will affect our working relationship?
- What would be the advantages of solving the problem ourselves?



In the long term, empowering people to think through the natural consequences of a solution will pay off for the working relationship. Forcing or overpowering them will just as predictably damage the relationship and often will produce results that will backfire.

### Exercise 5.5

Recall the political situation you identified in Exercise 2.2 (page 17), and answer the following questions.

1. What, if any, overpowering tactics have you or your partner in this situation used on each other to date?

   ________________________________________

   ________________________________________

2. What questions can you ask to use the "power of the problem" to persuade your partner to agree to a mutually beneficial solution?

   ________________________________________

   ________________________________________

## INVEST IN YOUR RELATIONSHIP "TRUST FUND"

Trust is often what makes relationships succeed or fail. Even the most difficult problems are easier to resolve when two people trust each other.

The amount of trust in your relationships with people at work can be pictured as a trust fund. You invest in and increase the balance of the trust fund by being trustworthy yourself. You deplete your trust fund by being untrustworthy and undependable. Trust funds are built up or drawn down by your day-to-day interactions with your political partners. Unfortunately, it seems to be much easier to make a big withdrawal than it is to make a big investment. If you want to have a trusting relationship with others, you must avoid withdrawals and consistently make investments.

Trust is based on two ingredients: credibility and competence. We trust people who do what they say they will do—that is, when they are credible. We also trust people when we are confident that they have the knowledge and skill necessary to get the job done—that is, when they are competent.

Here are some tips on how to *make credibility investments* and *avoid withdrawals:*



**1. Be clear.** When you say that you *may* be able to finish a project by Monday, your partner may hear that you *will* be able to finish it by then. You need to be clear and specific about what you are (and are not) willing to commit to. For example, if you are not certain that you will be able to finish the project by Monday, you need to explain, "I may be able to finish the project by Monday, but I cannot guarantee that it will be done before Wednesday morning."

**2. Keep your promises.** Few things destroy trust as much as broken promises. If you want good working relationships, you need to think carefully before making promises.

**3. Be honest.** You cannot collaborate effectively with someone who is dishonest. If you want to be trusted, you must be honest. Being honest does not mean that you have to tell everyone everything you know. There may be instances when you cannot share things you know because you have promised to keep the information confidential. In these instances, it is wise to tell the person that you cannot discuss a particular topic and explain why you cannot do so.

To *make competence investments* and *avoid withdrawals:*

**1. Do not fake competence when the stakes are high.** It is good to walk at the edge of your competence. Being willing to take risks is critical to expanding your abilities. But when there are high stakes at risk, do not try to fool your partner into thinking you are capable when you are not. You may luck out and succeed—this time. But if you do not, it will take a long time to build your trust fund back up with this partner.

**2. Leverage your personal strengths.** People succeed by building on their strengths, not by continually working on their weaknesses. You will be a more effective working partner if you seek out situations well suited to your unique talents and skills.

**3. Accurately assess your partner's capabilities.** Make sure your partner knows how to do what you are trusting him or her to do. For example, if your subordinate has never done a market survey before, it is unwise to trust him or her to do it correctly without any supervision. Do not put your partner in a situation where he or she is doomed to fail. The balance in your trust fund will drop dramatically.



**4. Take calculated risks on your partner's competence.** Often you make agreements to allow others to complete projects or tasks on your behalf, but you fail to trust them to do the job right—even though they have a successful track record on similar projects. Instead, you try to maintain control over what they are doing and how they are doing it. People who feel controlled become passive and end up needing even more control. This spiral continues until you are exhausted from all your controlling and they are completely frustrated by their lack of autonomy and initiative. You need to ask yourself, "Am I not trusting them because they are untrustworthy or because I cannot let go of control?" If it is the latter, you need to back off and let your partners do their job.

**5. When your partner makes a mistake, focus on the problem, not the person.** How do you respond when someone makes a mistake or fails to follow through on a commitment? Do you make it clear that the individual is to blame for the problem (and that you are blameless)? This approach makes people defensive. When problems arise in the future, your partner will be tempted to cover them up instead of bringing them to your attention. Help him or her be honest by focusing on how to keep the problem from happening again, rather than making sure that the "guilty" party is punished.

Applying these tips to her situation with Charlie, Chris needs to audit her trust fund. What has she done to make credibility investments? Has she kept her promises? Has she said things about Charlie to others that may get back to him, thus giving him the clear message that he cannot count on her to be honest with him? What has she done to make competence investments in her trust fund with Charlie? Has she faked competence? Has she trusted his competence—appropriately or inappropriately? When Charlie has made mistakes, how has she responded? Has she focused on the problem or the person?

Chris also needs to separate her disagreement with Charlie from her trust in him. They have a legitimate disagreement about the best way to submit customer orders. Both may claim that the problem is a lack of trust. But the true problem is that neither of them is willing to alter the way orders are processed and shipped. Lack of trust is making it more difficult for them to solve this problem, but even if Chris and Charlie trusted each other completely, they would still have a problem. Chris must focus on solving this problem. If she does this by playing positive politics, the trust between Charlie and her will grow.

## Exercise 5.6



Recall the political challenge you identified in Exercise 2.2 (page 17), and answer the following questions.

**1.** What have you done in this situation that may have reduced your trust fund with your partner? Was it a credibility or a competence withdrawal?

______________________________________________

______________________________________________

**2.** What has your partner done that has reduced your trust? Was it a credibility or a competence withdrawal?

______________________________________________

______________________________________________

**3.** What can you start doing immediately to increase your trust fund with your partner?

______________________________________________

______________________________________________

**4.** What can you do to help your partner become more trustworthy?

______________________________________________

______________________________________________

# Chapter Checkpoints

Great work relationships do not develop overnight. They take time and hard work. The secret to building great work relationships is to follow these six principles:

✓ Assert yourself by standing up for your needs and interests.

✓ Use your head and your heart to stay fully involved in the problem and the relationship.

✓ Respect and understand your partner to avoid making him or her defensive and to create collaborative solutions to the conflict.

✓ Communicate directly and proactively to keep channels open and clear.

✓ Empower your partner to choose by using the "power of the problem" to persuade rather than overwhelm him or her.

✓ Invest in your relationship "trust fund" by making credibility and competence investments.

CHAPTER

# 6 Dealing with Negative Politics

**This chapter will help you to:**

- Recognize negative political strategies.
- Understand why people use negative political tactics.
- Learn to reach satisfactory agreements with negative political politicians.

## NEGATIVE POLITICAL TACTICS

When you encounter a political situation, you usually choose a political strategy—avoidance, accommodation, competition, compromise, or collaboration—that fits your goals in the situation. Your political tactics—the political actions that you take—are largely determined by the political strategies that you and your partners adopt. If you choose uncollaborative political strategies, the result usually is *negative political tactics.* The ongoing story of Chris and Charlie illustrates this point.

**Shipping and the Surly Sales Representative: Part IV**

Having decided that her problem with Charlie had a high priority, Chris thought about how to proceed. Her first concern was that Charlie was not the only person involved who was not playing positive politics.

- Eric, her supervisor, had been no help at all. He seemed unwilling to risk any confrontation with the sales department. Chris thought to herself, "Eric probably believes that I will fail to reach an accord with Charlie, and he does not want to be tainted with my failure. He thinks the best thing he can do to advance his career is to avoid this conflict."

- Juan, Chris's shipping clerk, had been very supportive of her. Chris had suggested several ways for Juan to work more effectively with Charlie, and Juan had enthusiastically implemented each of Chris's suggestions. Unfortunately, none had worked. "The problem with Juan," Chris reflected, "is that he agrees with me too quickly. He never offers any suggestions of his own. I know he's a very bright individual. I'm sure he has some ideas about how to deal with Charlie. But he seems to worry that he will offend me if he suggests an idea that I haven't thought of on my own. I need to encourage him to give me his recommendations."

- Charlie continued to show little concern for Chris or her problems. "He thinks I'll be fired if I don't give in to him, so he has little incentive to deal with me. I have to convince him that he's better off dealing with me than with someone else. I need to prove to him that I can best take care of him and his customers, provided he works with me."

- Deanna, Charlie's supervisor, seemed sincerely interested in helping Chris reach an agreement with Charlie. "I appreciate her cooperative spirit," Chris said to herself. "She suggested that Charlie complete his paperwork twice a week, on Wednesday afternoons and Saturdays, instead of just once a week. But we still won't be able to make the shipping deadline for customers who submit their orders to Charlie on Monday or Thursday."

Chris wondered how she could get these four people to work more effectively on resolving their conflicts. ■

## Exercise 6.1

Recall the five political strategies from Chapter 3. Think about the tactics used by each of Chris's political partners, then try to match each person with his or her political strategy.

| | |
|---|---|
| Charlie | Accommodator |
| Chris | Avoider |
| Deanna | Collaborator |
| Eric | Competitor |
| Juan | Compromiser |

Charlie is the competitor. His only concern is making sure that his interests are satisfied. Chris is the collaborator. She wants a solution that will satisfy everyone's interests, including her own. Deanna is the compromiser. She has suggested that both Charlie and Chris give in a little, but the solution she offers will not meet either of their needs. Eric is the avoider. He is completely unwilling to engage the sales department in conflict, even if it means that his department's performance suffers as a result. Finally, Juan is the accommodator. He has been so concerned about maintaining a good relationship with Chris that he has been unwilling to disagree with any of her suggestions for dealing with Charlie or to offer any suggestions of his own.

# WHY PEOPLE ADOPT NEGATIVE POLITICAL STRATEGIES

Why is it that some people decide to collaborate, while others choose to play unproductive political games? People's political strategies and tactics are determined by how they think and feel about a political situation. If they perceive that the forces for collaboration are stronger than the forces against it, they will collaborate. Otherwise, they will use negative political tactics. The "forcefield" diagram below illustrates some of the forces for and against collaboration.

| FORCES FOR COLLABORATION | FORCES AGAINST COLLABORATION |
|---|---|
| "I want to satisfy my interests." → | ← "It's a win-lose world." |
| "I need to work with others to get what I want." → | ← "Competition brings out the best in people." |
| "I have confidence in my own problem-solving skills." → | ← "Collaboration is not the way we do things here." |
| | ← "Things can only get worse." |
| "I have confidence in my political partners' problem-solving skills." → | ← "People will take advantage of me." |
| "All of us will have to work together again in the future." → | ← "I won't be an effective political player." |



### Exercise 6.2

Think about the last time you tried to negotiate with a difficult political partner. What beliefs and fears caused your partner to adopt a negative political strategy?

## COUNTERING NEGATIVE POLITICAL TACTICS

Your best bet for countering your partner's negative political tactics is to weaken the forces against collaboration. If you can help him or her understand that collaboration is the best way to deal with others, or if you can reduce his or her fears of collaboration, your partner will be much less likely to employ negative tactics.

Assume that your co-workers demand that you do something for them that will take a lot of your time, but they refuse to help you deal with the work overload that this will create. They explain that, in the past, people have taken advantage of them in situations like this. This fear that people will take advantage of them has led them to play negative politics. If you can reduce this fear by assuring your co-workers that you really want to satisfy their interests, you may be able to convince them to collaborate with you.

Or take the case of the co-worker who always agrees to do whatever you want and never shares his or her own suggestions and opinions. People like this may be afraid that you will not want to work with them if they offer suggestions that you do not agree with. You can weaken this fear by assuring them that you will continue to work with them in the future, as long as they collaborate in good faith with you.

## Exercise 6.3

Consider the difficult political partner whose beliefs and fears you described in Exercise 6.2. What might you do to bring a halt to his or her negative political tactics?

____________________________________________________________

____________________________________________________________

____________________________________________________________

In many ways, negative politics is like an evil spirit that creates dissension and poor relationships within a community. People in some societies believe that the first step in dealing with evil spirits is to name them. Naming an evil spirit is thought to take away its power and mystique.

In a similar manner, naming your partner's negative political tactics can help you unfreeze your negotiations. The following four-step procedure may help you gain victory over the negative tactics you encounter:

**1. Identify the tactic.** What is your partner doing to block or resist solving the problem?

**2. Name the tactic.** This must be done tactfully, using neutral, descriptive language. If you name the tactic using evaluative or threatening language—"I'm tired of the way you ignore everything I say, and I'm not going to stand for it any more!"—your partner is likely to become defensive. If you describe the tactic in neutral terms—"I think I understand your interests here, but you seem unwilling to listen to my interests and concerns. If that's true, I need to hear why you feel that way. Could you explain why to me?"—you will set the tone for a rational, productive discussion. The table on pages 66–67 provides examples of how to name commonly used negative political tactics.

**3. Let your partner respond.** Be quiet. Give your partner time to respond. There may be a silence so lengthy that it makes you nervous. You may be tempted to fill the silence by offering an explanation of your partner's tactics. This is the *wrong* thing to do. Suffer in silence for a few moments, if you must, but do not put words in your partner's mouth.

**4. Deal with your partner's concerns.** Find out what beliefs or fears are preventing your partner from collaborating with you. Then deal with these concerns. Help your partner to understand the benefits of collaboration. Reduce his or her fears of working with you.

## Exercise 6.4



Think about the negative political tactics you identified in Exercise 6.2. How could you describe these tactics *in neutral terms* for your partner?

________________________________________

________________________________________

________________________________________

**NAMING NEGATIVE POLITICAL TACTICS**

| Political Strategy | Political Tactic | Naming the Tactic |
|---|---|---|
| Avoidance | Silence—your political partner is silent or says very little | "You are very quiet. I am not sure how to interpret your silence. Will you please share your thoughts with me?" |
| | Changing the subject—your partner keeps changing the subject | "The subject keeps shifting, Could we stay focused on this problem for now?" |
| Accommodation | Compliance—your partner agrees to do whatever you request | "You seem to be willing to agree to anything that I say. I'd like to hear your thoughts about this." |
| | Martyr—your partner agrees to do what you want, even though it will cost him or her dearly | "You seem to have some serious reservations about the solutions that we've been discussing. I'd like to hear what your concerns are." |
| Competition | Attack—your partner attacks you | "You seem to be upset about something I am doing. Can you tell me what you are angry about?" |
| | Bullying—your partner threatens or intimidates you | "Whenever I raise this issue, you tell me that you may have to tell our vice president about it. This feels like a threat. If it is, please explain why you feel the need to threaten me." |

| Political Strategy | Political Tactic | Naming the Tactic |
|---|---|---|
| Compromise | Milking concessions—after the deal is closed, your partner asks for ''one more thing'' | ''It seems to me that you're trying to add something new to our agreement. If that's true, we'll need to review all the elements of the deal before going any further. How would you like to proceed?'' |
| | Splitting the difference—your partner suggests that you solve the problem by both giving in a little | ''You seem to be ready to settle for a compromise solution. Will that fully meet all of your needs? Which needs will that leave unfulfilled?'' |

# Chapter Checkpoints

✓ Negative political tactics often result from uncollaborative political strategies.

✓ People are more likely to employ positive, collaborative political tactics if the forces against collaboration are weakened.

✓ Deal directly with a difficult partner's negative political tactics:

1. Identify the tactic.
2. Name the tactic, using neutral, descriptive language.
3. Let your partner respond.
4. Deal with your partner's concerns.

CHAPTER

# 7 Engaging Avoiders

**This chapter will help you to:**

- Know why the avoider employs negative tactics.
- Recognize the avoider's favorite political tactics.
- Learn how you can counter the avoider's tactics.

## AVOIDANCE STRATEGY AND TACTICS

The avoiders' motto is "Things can only get worse." Consequently, they shun politics and power. They believe that politics is bad because it usually produces results they do not like. They think they are the only ones capable of taking care of themselves and their needs, and they fear that others will take advantage of them.

Avoiders rarely expect to satisfy their own interests, so they hope to maintain a somewhat comfortable status quo. And avoiders have no desire to build positive working relationships. Most avoiders would rather hide in their offices.

## Exercise 7.1

Think of the avoiders you have known. What attitudes, beliefs, and fears have caused them to adopt the avoider strategy?

________________________________________

________________________________________

________________________________________

The continuing story of Chris and Charlie illustrates how frustrating it can be to deal with an avoider.



### Shipping and the Surly Sales Representative: Part V

Chris met with Eric to discuss her plans for dealing with Charlie. She showed Eric the list of Charlie's needs and interests that she had prepared. Eric agreed that it was quite thorough. "Now what I need to do," Chris explained, "is find a solution that will satisfy Charlie's interests *and* ours." Eric nodded in agreement.

Chris continued, "Because Charlie can be so difficult, I may need your help to solve this problem with him." Chris noticed Eric squirm in his chair. "Eric, Charlie has a habit of attacking people and then walking away whenever he feels threatened. If he does that to me—if he attacks me and refuses to talk about the shipping problem with me—I may need you to talk with Charlie's boss, Deanna. Would you be willing to ask Deanna to tell Charlie that he has to work with me on this problem?"

Eric replied, "Chris, this is *your* problem. I want *you* to figure out a way to solve it. That's why I hired you as the shipping supervisor; I don't have time to deal with all the day-to-day problems of the shipping room."

Chris spent 10 minutes trying to convince Eric to support her if she needed help, but she got nowhere.

Chris had lunch the next day with Jake Saveson, a long-time company employee who worked in the factory. Jake laughed, "Charlie's a character, all right. About five years ago, before your time, Eric had your job. He and Charlie got in a bad run-in over a shipping problem with Charlie's biggest account. Eric said it was Charlie's fault, Charlie said it was Eric's, and they got into a huge shouting match out by the shipping dock. I thought they were going to duke it out. The whole place was talking about it. Well, the next day, the president of the company stomps down to Eric's office, slams the door, and reads Eric the riot act. He tells Eric never to forget that Shipping takes its orders from Sales. He says, 'Eric, if I ever hear about you making trouble for one of our sales reps again, you're fired. And I will personally sign your pink slip!' I guess Eric's still a little scared about crossing swords with Charlie." Jake continued to chuckle.

Now Chris understood why Eric was so reluctant to help her. She wondered, "How can I convince Eric to intervene with Sales if I need his help? And what contingency plans should I make in case Eric is unwilling to help me?" ■



Avoiders such as Eric refuse to get involved in workplace politics. Avoiders tend to sit on the sidelines and let others battle. Eric's behavior illustrates some of the most common negative political tactics used by avoiders: detachment, irritability, pretending to go along, and distraction.

## DETACHMENT

### Recognizing Detachment

Avoiders who have been beaten up by politics often decide that the best tactic is detachment—staying out of politics altogether. You can recognize detached people by their stooped shoulders (from carrying the weight of the world) and their grim expressions. You often hear them say things like:

- "It's not my job."
- "It's too hard."
- "I don't care how things turn out."
- "I can't make a difference. No matter what I do, things won't turn out my way."

In the story of Chris and Charlie, Eric tried to detach himself from a political situation by telling Chris that it was not *his* responsibility to deal with Charlie.

## Countering Detachment

When partners try to detach themselves from your problems, you may feel like telling them "Wake up and smell the coffee!" "This is your problem as much as mine!" Obviously, this is not the best way to deal with detachment. Your anger will only reinforce the avoider's belief that he or she always gets beat up in political situations.

Fortunately, there are several ways to counter detachment:

1. **Make your partner feel safe.** Begin with small agreements. If you are wrestling with a very complex problem and your partner refuses to get involved, choose a small piece of the problem and agree on a solution. Then follow through on the commitments you make. This will increase your trust fund with your partner, and later you will be able to tap into the fund when you need to negotiate a solution to the rest of the problem.

2. **Boost your partner's confidence.** Cite examples of past achievements. Make your partner aware of his or her power to help the organization achieve its goals.

3. **Get your partner to take responsibility for the desired results.** Detachment is a favorite tactic of people who fear losing control of a situation. Often they will acknowledge your problems and agree with your goals, but they will refuse to help you because they fear you will manipulate them to your advantage. So let them take charge of the problem! Ask them to suggest solutions. Put your services at their disposal. Ask what support they need from you.

4. **Explain the consequences of failing to negotiate.** If all else fails, tell your partner about your insurance policy. Your detached partner may believe that there will be no cost to withholding help. Explain what actions you will take if you do not receive support. Make him or her aware that if you have to use your insurance policy, he or she may be much worse off than at present. Illustrate how a negotiated solution would be better for *both* of you because everyone's needs would be satisfied.

## Exercise 7.2

1. When was the last time a political partner used the detachment tactic with you? What did your partner say or do?

   ______________________________________________

   ______________________________________________

2. How did you respond to the detachment?

   ______________________________________________

   ______________________________________________

3. How could you have handled the situation more positively?

   ______________________________________________

   ______________________________________________

# IRRITABILITY

## Recognizing Irritability

Some avoiders develop prickly personalities so people will leave them alone. They snap and snarl at people. Or they give people the silent treatment. Often they wear a nasty expression around the office that warns people, "Stay away! I'm in a ba-a-a-a-a-ad mood!"

You may hear stories indicating that these people have a completely different personality outside of work—they do volunteer work in homeless shelters, they coach Little League teams, they help raise money for medical research. You wonder how they developed their Jekyll-and-Hyde personality. The answer is that their irritability forms a protective shell around them at work. It helps them avoid bruising political battles, which often cost them dearly.

## Countering Irritability

The two most common—and equally *in*effective—countermoves for dealing with irritability are (1) walking away and (2) responding in kind. Neither of these countermoves serves your interests; both fail to get what you need from your partner.

To counter irritability, you need to engage the other person in a discussion of your problems. You need to prevent the irritability from distracting you from your goals. Here are four pointers:

**1. Stay cool.** Do not let your partner's irritability goad you into an angry, defensive, or irritable response. Keep your temper. Do not take the irritability personally, even if your partner attacks you directly.

**2. Acknowledge your partner's feelings.** Do not try to convince your partner that "life is not all that bad." This will just put your partner on the defensive. It is important to understand that your partner's complaints reflect valid feelings. Acknowledging these feelings—by active listening or by writing them on a white board—will show your partner you care about his or her concerns.

**3. Turn personal attacks into problem-solving opportunities.** In the midst of your partner's snapping and snarling, your partner may direct a few cheap shots toward you. This is an excellent opportunity to turn your partner toward problem solving. Instead of responding in anger, tell your partner, "I'm sorry that I upset you. What can we do to fix this problem?"

**4. Ask problem-solving questions.** In *Getting Past No: Negotiating with Difficult People* (New York: Bantam, 1991), William Ury notes that one of the best ways to get people to address a problem is to ask them about it. Rather than telling an irritable person, "We've got a problem and this is what I think we should do about it," it is better to solicit his or her impressions of the problem. "What is the problem? Why is this a problem? How is it affecting you in your job? What things would you like to see changed? How would you make these changes? What would be wrong with doing things this way?"

## Exercise 7.3

1. When was the last time you dealt with an irritable political partner? What did your partner say or do?

   ______________________________

   ______________________________

2. How did you respond to your partner's irritability?

   ______________________________

   ______________________________

**3.** How could you have handled the situation more positively?

______________________________________________

______________________________________________

# PRETENDING TO GO ALONG

## Recognizing Pretending to Go Along

Perhaps the most frustrating avoider tactic is "pretending to go along." The partner who employs this tactic will listen to your problem, assure you that he or she is your best friend in the world, and pledge to support you through thick and thin—but never follow through on these promises. If you go back to your partner a couple of weeks later to ask what happened, "Oh, gee, I'm sorry! I forgot all about that. I feel terrible. What can I do to make it up to you?" He or she will make a note to do what you have asked but will never get around to it.

People who pretend to go along often appear very sincere. They charm and calm you when you confront them about their failure to keep commitments. Those who pretend to go along hope that, in time, you will forget what you have asked them to do. That way, they will not have to get involved in your political battles.



## Countering Pretending to Go Along

To deal effectively with this tactic, you need to develop some backbone. You need to let your partner know that you value his or her friendship but that you insist on trustworthy and dependable behavior.

**1. Name the tactic.** Your partner's tactic is to stall you as long as possible. If you recognize the game but wait several days or weeks before saying anything about it, you are playing into your partner's hand. Describe your partner's game in neutral language. "You have made three commitments that you failed to keep. What can we do to make sure that this doesn't happen again?"

**2. Insist on fairness.** Say that it is unfair to make promises and commitments that your partner does not intend to keep. Make it clear why you need help to satisfy your interests. Assure him or her that you want to be fair. Say "Tell me what your interests are in this situation and how I can help you satisfy those interests."

**3. Jointly establish objective standards.** Do not settle for a handshake and your partner's pledge to "take care of things this time." Insist upon objective standards that can be used to determine whether you and your partner are both living up to the agreement. These standards might include target dates for completing tasks, quality standards, expert reviews, or expense limits.

**4. Explain the consequences of failing to follow through on agreements.** Let your partner know what will happen if he or she fails to keep his or her commitments.

- How will your partner's actions affect you and others who work with you? Will it mean that you and your co-workers have to spend the next several weekends making up for the work your partner failed to do?
- How will your partner's actions affect the problem you are trying to solve? For example, will they delay a new program, costing the company thousands or millions of dollars?
- What will happen to your partner if agreements aren't met? Will you let your partner's supervisor know that he or she has not kept those commitments? Will you withdraw support for a project? Will you attempt to recover your expenses from his or her budget?



All of these countermoves will help your partners see that they cannot count on your friendship and goodwill to keep them out of trouble if they only pretend to go along.

## Exercise 7.4

1. When was the last time you had to deal with a political partner who was pretending to go along? What did your partner say or do?

______________________________________________

______________________________________________

2. How did you respond to your partner's behavior? How long did it take before you "named the game"?

______________________________________________

______________________________________________

3. How could you have handled the situation more positively?

______________________________________________

______________________________________________

# DISTRACTION

## Recognizing Distraction

Distraction is one of the most sophisticated avoider tactics. Distractors will suggest long, complex approaches to solving problems. "Let's conduct a detailed study!" they tell you. "We'll convene an interdepartmental task force, hire a world-famous consultant, and attend an educational seminar together in three or four months." Actually, the problems could be solved in a couple of hours if the distractors would agree to roll up their sleeves and tackle the problem with you. Like the avoiders who pretend to go along, distractors want to put you off. They hope you will get so caught up in the problem-solving process that you will forget all about solving the problem! That way, they will not have to spend any time helping you.

## Countering Distraction



To counter distraction, stay focused on your interests. Here are some pointers:

1. **Do not take the bait.** Keep your conversation with your partner focused on the problem at hand; do not allow yourself to be sidetracked from your real interests.

2. **Cut the game off quickly.** Have you ever gotten started on a small home improvement project that turned into a budget-breaking major renovation? Going into the project you told yourself, "This is how much I can afford to spend on this improvment. It is not worth it for me to spend any more." But once you became invested in the project—financially and psychologically—you spent far more than you intended. The same thing can happen in political battles with distractors. It is therefore important to cut the game off early and remind your political partner of the true priorities.

3. **Address your partner's concerns and fears.** Avoiders do not play the distraction game unless they are concerned about something. You must address any concerns, or the avoider will continue to interfere with your work. Get together with your partners, determine what is troubling them, and help find a solution to their problems.

4. **Establish cost and scheduling standards.** People who employ distraction tactics often act as if time and money do not matter. "Let's leave

no stone unturned. A job worth doing is worth doing well. Quality must be our highest priority." If you argue with any of these clichés, you risk sounding like you are not concerned about slipshod work. Instead of arguing against quality, it is better to reply, "Yes, quality is important, and doing a quality job means that we must stay within budget and on schedule as we complete our work. Do you have any suggestions that will help us meet *all* of our quality standards?"

## Exercise 7.5

**1.** When was the last time you had to deal with a political partner who played the distraction game? What did your partner say or do?

______________________________

______________________________

**2.** How did you respond to your partner's behavior? Were you able to cut the game off quickly?

______________________________

______________________________



**3.** How could you have handled the situation more positively?

______________________________

______________________________

# Chapter Checkpoints

✓ Avoiders shun politics because they usually lose political contests and they fear that "things can only get worse."

✓ Four of the most common political tactics employed by avoiders are detachment, irritability, pretending to go along, and distraction.

✓ Countermoves against avoiders create an environment where avoiders feel that it is safe and fruitful to express their interests and to negotiate an agreement.

CHAPTER

# 8 Toughening Accommodators

**This chapter will help you to:**

- See why the accommodator employs negative tactics instead of collaborating.
- Recognize the accommodator's favorite political tactics.
- Learn how you can counter accommodator tactics.

## ACCOMMODATION STRATEGY AND TACTICS

Accommodators believe that nothing is more important than maintaining friendly relationships between people. When political conflicts grow intense, you may hear the accommodator say, "If we all make an effort to get along, I'm sure everything will be OK."

Like avoiders, accommodators have little desire to satisfy their own interests. But *unlike* avoiders, accommodators are very interested in satisfying others. They will gladly participate in politics if their participation will help create harmony and build personal relationships.

## Exercise 8.1

Think of the accommodators you have known. What were some of the attitudes, beliefs, and fears that turned them into accommodators?

________________________________________

________________________________________

________________________________________

In the continuing story of Chris and Charlie, note how Juan attempts to accommodate Chris and how much frustration this causes her.

### Shipping and the Surly Sales Representative: Part VI

Chris and Juan were brainstorming ideas for dealing with Charlie. "I think there are three things we have to be concerned about as we try to reach an agreement with Charlie," Chris said. "First, we have achieved 99 percent shipping accuracy for our other sales reps' customers. We need to achieve the same accuracy for Charlie's customers. Second, if we make special arrangements with Charlie for sending us orders, we need to offer those same arrangements to the other sales reps. Otherwise, we'll have a rebellion. Third, we cannot agree to any solution that will cost us more money, because there is no extra money available in our budget. Have you identified any other concerns, Juan?"

Juan looked at his list of concerns. It was a full page long and contained several items that Chris had not mentioned, but Juan shook his head no.

Chris could see that Juan had made a very long list. "Juan, are you sure there's nothing you wish to add to my list of concerns?"

Juan replied, "Your list is very comprehensive, as usual."

After a few seconds Chris said, "I just thought of another concern, Juan. I think our solution should not cause any layoffs or firings in the shipping department."

"Yes," Juan agreed, "I have that on my list, too."

"And another thing," Chris added. "We need to make sure the solution does not have an adverse effect on customer satisfaction with shipping."

"Yes, that is also on my list."

Chris glared at Juan. "Juan, why don't you just tell me what's on your list?" Juan shrugged. "So," Chris said, "does this mean we're going to have to sit here until I've guessed every single concern on your list? Wouldn't it be more efficient if you just read your list to me?"

Juan is so worried about damaging his relationship with Chris that he is afraid to voice his concerns to her. He does not realize that his accommodation strategy is far more damaging to their relationship than open, honest communication.

The conversation between Chris and Juan illustrates that, even though it seems like it would be easy to negotiate with an accommodator, it actually can be quite frustrating. Unless you are a mind reader, you never know for sure what the accommodator wants. This always leaves you wondering if the accommodator will be able to live with the negotiated solution that you develop together. ■



Accommodators use a variety of different political tactics. The most common tactics include obsequiousness, smile-and-denial, blind trust, and martyrdom.

# OBSEQUIOUSNESS

## Recognizing Obsequiousness

Obsequiousness is a $64,000 word that describes someone who is fawning, overly deferential, and far too compliant. Obsequious accommodators cannot say no because they want desperately to be liked, and are afraid people will not like them if they turn down requests or disagree with others. Obsequious individuals seemingly have no interests of their own, except a desire to stay in everyone's good graces.

## Countering Obsequiousness

The key to countering obsequiousness is to create an environment where the obsequious individual feels safe speaking up. There are several countermoves that are particularly effective:

**1. Enhance your partner's self-confidence.** Tell your partner that his or her opinions and interests are very important to you. Assure your partner that speaking up will not jeopardize your relationship and that it will increase your respect.

**2. Ask open-ended questions.** Ask open-ended questions that allow your partner to offer opinions. "Why do you think it would be a good idea to add a third shift? Why not simply hire more employees for the two existing shifts? What if we offered our current employees an incentive to become more productive?" If at all possible, ask such questions *before* you offer your own opinions.

**3. Establish a "no criticism" period.** Obsequious partners dread criticism. They take criticism to be the same as personal disapproval. Consequently, they are likely to clam up as soon as someone criticizes one of their ideas. Establishing a "no criticism" period, when anyone can describe his or her interests and offer suggestions and ideas without fear of criticism or disapproval, will encourage open communication. Be sure to thank your obsequious partners for sharing their ideas with you.



**4. Explain how obsequiousness will affect the relationship.** If your partner continues to be obsequious, explain that this will have a negative impact on your relationship. Stress that you are not interested in maintaining a relationship unless it is open and honest.

### Exercise 8.2

1. When was the last time a political partner was obsequious around you? What did your partner say or do?

   ___

   ___

2. How did you respond to the obsequiousness?

   ___

   ___

**3.** How could you have handled the situation more positively?

_______________________________________________

_______________________________________________

# SMILE-AND-DENIAL

## Recognizing Smile-and-Denial

Many accommodators dislike conflict intensely. It makes them nervous. They spend much of their time trying to smooth over problems instead of solving them. "We don't have a problem here." "Let's play nice with each other." "There is no problem so great that our relationship can't overcome it." "Let's all shake hands and make up." This accommodator tactic is known as "smile-and-denial."

## Countering Smile-and-Denial



You may be tempted to hide disagreements from people who play the smile-and-denial game because conflict makes them so uncomfortable. Don't! It is important to show these people that conflict *can* bring people together. Here are three pointers:

**1. Keep your temper.** Flashes of temper will evoke the smile-and-denial tactic from political partners who fear conflict. If you can keep an even temper, your partner is much less likely to fear that your relationship is in jeopardy.

**2. Stay focused on the problem.** Do not let the smile-and-denial tactic sidetrack you from problem solving. Even if you lose your temper and find that you need some time apart from your partner to regain your emotional balance, make sure you and your partner get back together to work out a solution to your problem.

**3. Reconfirm the relationship.** The greatest fear of people who employ the smile-and-denial tactic is that conflict will destroy relationships. To quell this fear, reconfirm the relationship during your negotiations. For example, you can say, "I know this is difficult for both of us, but I appreciate your willingness to discuss these issues openly with me. It gives me a lot of confidence that we can solve any problems we encounter in the future."

### Exercise 8.3

1. When was the last time your political partner tried to minimize an important problem you were trying to solve? What did your partner say or do?

   ______________________________

   ______________________________

2. How did you respond to your partner's "smile-and-denial"?

   ______________________________

   ______________________________

3. How could you have handled the situation more positively?

   ______________________________

   ______________________________

# BLIND TRUST



## Recognizing Blind Trust

Some accommodators decide to hitch their star to an individual they greatly admire. Much as Robin was loyal to Batman and Tonto put his faith in the Lone Ranger, these accommodators blindly trust their interests will be protected by their patron. They go to great lengths to maintain this relationship, never crossing swords with their patron even on minor issues. Everything they say is twisted to protect their patron's interests.

Dealing with people who employ the blind trust tactic can be extremely frustrating. No matter how much you plead with them, they will not share their own opinions, thoughts, and ideas with you. And, if you happen to be the patron whom they admire, you are always worried that they are telling you what they think you want to hear instead of what you need to hear.

## Countering Blind Trust

It may prove very difficult for you to deal with blind trust—especially if you are the object of that trust. Trust is very flattering. It boosts your ego and enhances your self-esteem. But blind trust can be frustrating because it gets in the way of open communication. Here are some countermoves:

**1. Find out what blind trust accommodators care about.** It is impossible to know the interests of people who blindly trust others, in part because they often have trouble distinguishing their own interests from those of their patrons. They may be unwilling or unable to tell you how they personally would like to see work problems resolved; their views are shaped almost totally by their patrons. However, you can probe to find out what sorts of job responsibilities they want, their career goals, their work values, and so on. This probing will provide them with an opportunity to practice discussing their own interests and needs.

**2. Encourage openness.** Compliment blind trust accommodators when they speak their minds freely. Do not criticize their ideas, and do not subject their ideas to comparisons with their patrons' ideas. If you are their patron, make it clear that their free speech is strengthening your relationship.

**3. Reward honesty.** People who trust blindly find the idea of bearing bad news as intimidating as an ironman obstacle course. Thank them for sharing bad news honestly. Tell them how their honest behavior has helped you perform your job more effectively.

**4. Require blind trust accommodators to be independent.** When people trust you blindly, you need to create distance between you. Give them assignments that require them to operate independently. Make them speak their minds before offering your opinions. Reward them for acting independently, even if they are not entirely successful at first.



## Exercise 8.4

1. When was the last time you had to deal with a political partner who had blind trust in you? What did your partner say or do?

   ______________________________

   ______________________________

2. How did your partner's trust make you feel? How did you respond to your partner's behavior?

   ______________________________

   ______________________________

3. How could you have handled the situation more positively?

   ______________________________

   ______________________________

# MARTYRDOM

## Recognizing Martyrdom

We all know people who employ martyrdom tactics. They tell you they agree with all of your "insightful, fresh ideas," then the moment your back is turned they moan about how you will not listen to them. Or, worse yet, they stab you in the back by spreading rumors, sharing information you have told them in confidence, and criticizing you.

Martyrdom represents a unique accommodation tactic. In many respects, martyrs resemble those who play smile-and-denial games because they cannot stand conflict or confrontation. However, martyrs do not attach as much priority to maintaining relationships as do smile-and-denial people. In fact, martyrs often seek to distance themselves from agreements you have reached—agreements that do not represent their interests because they have been unwilling to share their interests with you. That is why martyrs are so quick to complain or plot against you when your back is turned.



## Countering Martyrdom

Martyrdom can endanger your interests. When you are the victim of rumors and lies, others may doubt your ability to keep agreements, and this may weaken your political power. As soon as you recognize martyrdom, you need to attack it:

**1. Name the tactic.** Tell the martyr you have heard that he or she is spreading rumors about you and criticizing you behind your back. Ask why he or she is doing these things.

**2. Address your partner's concerns and fears.** Recognize that the martyr's behavior is a sign that his or her interests are not being satisfied. Probe to uncover the concerns and fears that are prompting the martyr's behavior. Ask how you can address these concerns. If the martyr feels that you do not seek his or her input before making decisions, ask how you can gather his or her input more effectively.

**3. Specify expectations and consequences.** Tell the martyr that you do not want to see behavior like this in the future. Let the martyr know the consequences of this behavior. For example, will you inform supervisors about the behavior? Will you discuss the martyr's untrustworthy behavior with other colleagues, making it more difficult for the martyr to reach agreements with others?

**4. Reaffirm the relationship.** Let the martyr know that you value your relationship with him or her, but only if it is based on openness and honesty. Assure the martyr that you want to hear his or her views—even if they differ from yours—when you are trying to reach agreements.

## Exercise 8.5

1. When was the last time you were victimized by a martyr? What did this individual say or do?

   ______________________________

   ______________________________

2. How did you respond to the martyr's behavior? Did you confront him or her?

   ______________________________

   ______________________________

3. How could you have handled the situation more positively?

   ______________________________

   ______________________________

# Chapter Checkpoints

- ✓ Accommodators' principal political goal is to maintain harmonious relationships. Most accommodators cannot bear conflict.
- ✓ Four of the most common political tactics employed by accommodators are obsequiousness, smile-and-denial, blind trust, and martyrdom.
- ✓ Positive political countermoves help accommodators express their opinions honestly and deal with conflict constructively.

CHAPTER

# 9 Defusing Competitors

**This chapter will help you to:**

- Recognize the most common competitive tactics.
- Understand the beliefs and emotions that drive people to use competitive tactics.
- Learn how to counter competitive tactics with positive politics.

## COMPETITIVE STRATEGY AND TACTICS

Winning is the goal of the competitive strategy. When people choose to compete in a political situation, they concentrate on satisfying their own interests, often at the expense of others. People play competitive politics because:

- They fear that others will take advantage of them.
- They believe that resources (e.g., money, power, prestige) are limited or scarce, and want to get their share.
- They think a tough, competitive reputation will protect them against organizational "predators."
- They believe that competition "brings out the best" in people.
- They have competed successfully in similar situations in the past.
- They do not know another way to satisfy their interests.

## Exercise 9.1

We all compete in some of our interactions with others. Have you competed with someone at work in the past week? What drove you to choose this strategy? What were you thinking and feeling at the time?

________________________________________________

________________________________________________

________________________________________________

The key to dealing with competition is to defuse the underlying beliefs and fears with positive politics. For a firsthand view of a competitive strategy in action, let's return to Chris and Charlie.



### Shipping and the Surly Sales Representative: Part VII

Chris arranged to meet with Charlie at his field office. After a bumpy three-hour flight and problems in getting her baggage off the plane, Chris took a cab to Charlie's office. When the receptionist notified Charlie of Chris's arrival, he said he would be right out. Twenty minutes later he finally appeared in the lobby.

"Sorry about making you wait, Chris. I was on the phone with Megatron trying to calm them down about all these shipping errors. I'm glad you're here because I'm getting sick of having to spend my time on this problem. I hope you've come with some answers on how you're going to get it solved so I can get back to selling."

Chris was irritated that Charlie had made her wait so long, and no sooner had he opened his mouth than she felt the blood rush to her cheeks in anger. Taking several deep breaths to calm her nerves, she responded saying, "I'm glad we're getting the chance to meet in person about this, Charlie, and I'm confident we'll be able to come up with a solution that meets everyone's needs." The words sounded good, but she knew that Charlie was aware of the tension in her voice. His antenna for signs of emotion in others was ultrasensitive; unfortunately, he usually used the information to get his own way. ■

Even in this brief interaction in the lobby, Charlie clearly reveals his strategy for dealing with Chris. He is going to compete and will do whatever is necessary to ensure that he gets his own way. Some of the most common competitive tactics are one-upmanship, frontal attack, sabotage, and dirty tricks.

## ONE-UPMANSHIP

### Recognizing One-Upmanship

In playing one-upmanship, people act as if they are more important, more knowledgeable, or more confident than you, thus gaining a psychological edge. You know you are in a one-upmanship game when you feel like you are being pushed around, ignored, controlled, or put down. Charlie uses this tactic with Chris by making her wait. He sends her a clear message: "You are not my top priority; I've got bigger fish to fry!"



### Countering One-Upmanship

When this competitive tactic is used, you want to defend yourself. Depending on the circumstances, you may become angry and strike back or feel intimidated and give in. Either way, you get baited into playing negative politics.

Here are four things you can do to counter this tactic:

1. **Step back to see better.** Count to 10, take a break, breathe deeply 3 times—do *whatever* you need to keep or regain your emotional composure.

2. **Refocus on your interests.** Ask yourself, "What do I really care about here? What's really important to me?" One-upmanship is designed to get you worrying more about your self-image than about your interests.

**3. Build the competitor's self-confidence.** This seems like a crazy thing to do with someone who is trying to put you down. But it is important to understand that people are most likely to use one-upmanship when they are afraid that they may lose control of the situation. Psychologically, the root of this tactic is the fear that they may not have the knowledge, skill, or resources to cope. In other words, this tactic is about them, not about you. Focus on helping them feel more competent and you should see this tactic go away.

**4. When your interests are at stake, name the tactic.** Positive politics requires that you stand up for your interests. When you decide that one-upmanship is costing you too much time and emotional energy, name the tactic. Tell the person specifically what you see him or her doing (e.g., "Whenever I make a suggestion, you correct me in some way."). Explain how the behavior affects you and how you think it detracts from getting the problem solved. Press the competitor to set new ground rules for working together.

### Exercise 9.2

1. When was the last time someone used the one-upmanship tactic with you? What did the person say or do to try to put you in the "one-down" position?

   ______________________________

   ______________________________

2. How did you feel? How did you respond?

   ______________________________

   ______________________________

3. How could you have handled the situation more positively?

   ______________________________

   ______________________________



## FRONTAL ATTACK

## Recognizing the Frontal Attack

Recognizing the frontal attack will not be a problem. It is one of the competitor's favorite moves. Charlie launches his attack immediately in the lobby with Chris. His "apology" turns quickly into complaining about having to calm down a customer who is upset—again—because of shipping errors. He blames Chris and her department for the problem; he makes sure that he is viewed as the innocent, competent one who does not have to change his ways.

By attacking and blaming Chris, Charlie is trying to accomplish two things:

1. He wants to define the situation as a win–lose power struggle because history tells him he can win.
2. He wants to upset Chris because he has learned that, when upset, most people will strike back, give in, or run away. Since he believes he is more powerful, he is confident that he can repel any counter-attack and that he will get his way if Chris gives in or runs away.

## Countering the Frontal Attack

In countering the frontal attack, your first priority is to keep your reason and emotion in balance. Your best initial responses are to step back to gain perspective and get refocused on your interests. In addition, the following countermoves are helpful:

**1. "Let the wind blow."** There is an old Chinese saying that applies here: "If you want to get rid of something, you must first allow it to flourish." Rather than resist frontal attacks, encourage the attackers to keep on attacking. If they say that your proposal is stupid, ask them to tell you more about why they think it is stupid. If they blame you for a mistake, ask them—in a nondefensive tone—to tell you more about their view of why you are to blame. You do not have to agree; just encourage them to vent all their emotional energy before you respond.



**2. Refuse to play.** Arguing with someone who is frontally attacking you can weaken your political power and will not help either of you solve your problems.

**3. Neutralize the attack.** Once the attacker has vented most of his or her emotional energy, you can counter positively by reinterpreting the attack on you as an attack on the problem. For example, Chris could say to Charlie, "I can see that you really want to solve this problem, Charlie. Let's get started!"

**4. When the frontal attack persists, name the tactic.** Even more than one-upmanship, the frontal attack is a time-waster and an emotional drain. If your partner is a chronic attacker, then you need to name the tactic in neutral, descriptive terms and negotiate new ground rules for your working relationship.

### Exercise 9.3

1. When was the last time someone used the frontal attack with you? What did the person say or do to attack you?

_______________________________________________

_______________________________________________

2. How did you feel? How did you respond?

_______________________________________________

_______________________________________________

3. How could you have handled the situation more positively?

_______________________________________________

_______________________________________________

## SABOTAGE

### Recognizing Sabotage



Competitors use the sabotage tactic when they work to get what they want by undermining, going around, or going behind others. Sabotage can be conducted in many ways: spreading rumors, lobbying covertly to gain allies against others, holding meetings when adversaries are out of town or on vacation, withholding important information, loading meetings with supporters, using connections to gain an advantage, escalating a conflict immediately to a supportive boss, and so on.

Sabotage is one of the tactics most often associated with destructive politics in organizations. It often gets results—in the short term. But sabotage inevitably erodes trust and destroys relationships.

Because sabotage works best when the victim is unaware of what is going on, it is difficult to spot. And, if you spend a lot of energy worrying about sabotage, the paranoia will paralyze your efforts and poison your relationships.

A crossword-puzzle analogy may help you recognize sabotage in its early stages. Think about how an incorrect word in a crossword puzzle can lead you to put the wrong words in adjacent spaces. When you are being sabotaged, things people do or say (the words in the adjacent spaces) do not seem to add up because there are things happening that you do not know or have been misled about (the incorrect words).

## Countering Sabotage

The first step in countering sabotage is to recognize that it is happening. Once you know that you have been politically sabotaged, there are a number of things you need to do:

1. **Choose your battles.** Is this a battle worth fighting? When you accuse people of sabotage, you are entering emotionally charged territory and are in great danger of provoking a battle in which everyone will lose. Reassess what interests are at stake. If you will work with the saboteurs in the future, it is very important to confront them with your view of their behavior.

2. **Understand the saboteurs' interests.** People use sabotage as a way of satisfying their interests. What does the nature of the sabotage tell you about what these people care about? Have you taken all their interests into account in trying to come up with solutions to this problem or issue? Could you have prevented the sabotage by working harder to understand their interests and concerns? Have you stayed in close communication with them on these issues, even though the two of you disagree?

3. **Confront the saboteurs.** Sabotage works best in the shadows. When you have made the decision to confront your saboteurs, be direct, be specific, and do it right away. Name the game and ask them to help you understand why they felt this tactic was necessary. Help them understand the costs of their actions to your working relationship and to the task at hand. Make your initial confrontation a private one. If you feel you must make their actions public, inform them that you intend to do so.

4. **Beef up your security system.** Do you seem to get sabotaged often? If so, it may be that you need to be more assertive in building and maintaining a network of relationships with key people in your organization. This is *not* brown-nosing when it is done for the purpose of keeping an open line of communication for sharing interests, concerns, and ideas. Saboteurs typically need coconspirators to pull off their schemes. The stronger and more far-reaching your network of relationships, the more difficult it will be for a saboteur to draw others into a conspiracy against you.

## Exercise 9.4

1. When was the last time someone sabotaged you? What did the person say or do?

_______________________________________________

_______________________________________________

2. How did you feel? How did you respond?

_______________________________________________

_______________________________________________

3. How could you have handled the situation more positively?

_______________________________________________

_______________________________________________

# DIRTY TRICKS

## Recognizing a Dirty Trick

Like sabotage, the game of dirty tricks comes in as many different forms as the devious human brain can devise. A trick differs from sabotage in that the trickster deals directly with an adversary but says or does things that are misleading or untrue. Here is an example:



> Fred Lee's resentment of his former boss, Joanne Dupre, can be traced back to an event that occurred almost five years ago. He had caught wind of the possibility that the marketing manager's job in the consumer products division would be opening up soon. Hoping to get Joanne's support, he told her of his interest in the job and asked what he should do about it. She said she thought it would be a perfect job for him and that he could count on her support. Joanne promised that she would call Sandra Ben-Venisti, vice president of marketing, to discuss it with her. Two weeks later, Joanne was named the new marketing manager of the consumer products division.

Dirty tricks do not get much worse than this one. Fred went to Joanne to talk about a job possibility, trusting that she would help him out. Instead, she led him off the trail by saying she would talk to Sandra on his behalf; then she used the timely information Fred had given her to land a plum job for herself.

## Countering Dirty Tricks

Dirty tricks work only if you are fooled by them. The proactive way to deal with dirty tricks is to make yourself less vulnerable to deception. How can you do this?

**1. Work continuously to understand your partner's interests and concerns.** In the example above, Fred could have done a better job of staying abreast of Joanne's career goals and ambitions. If he had been better informed, he might have gone to someone else for support.

**2. Ask yourself if what the person is saying or doing is consistent with what you know about his or her interests.** If Fred had been aware of Joanne's interest in a job change, he could have asked himself whether her supporting his candidacy would be consistent with her own interests. He at least might have been aware of the possibility that her support for him would work against her own interest in getting the job.

**3. Ask yourself if the person is deceiving you by telling you what you want to believe.** Sometimes we are fooled by tricks because we really want to believe that what we are being told is true. And we usually want to hear good news—news that supports our interests and concerns. Fred wanted to hear that Joanne would support him and so was easily fooled when she told him she would.



Although these three steps can help reduce your vulnerability to tricks, inevitably there will be times when you will be caught by surprise. When that happens, the countermoves for dealing with the trick are similar to those for dealing with sabotage. Once you know that you have been politically tricked, you need to:

**1. Assess the costs and benefits of confrontation.** It is emotionally difficult to confront people about tricks they have played on you. Since they already have used the deception tactic, they are likely to deny or distort what happened, to invalidate your charge. Think hard about whether the costs of a confrontation are likely to be worth the benefits. Keep in mind that if you are likely to have to work with this person in the future, it is critical that you confront him or her.

**2. Create new solutions for addressing their interests.** Tricksters are trying to satisfy what they believe to be their interests. If you can come up with a more constructive, less deceptive, less costly way of satisfying them, you may be able to solve the substantive problem and establish a foundation for a more positive relationship in the future.

### 3. Confront the trickster.

- Be direct. Talk directly with the person who played the trick on you, not with anyone else about that person.
- Be specific. Tell the person exactly what you think he or she has done and the potential consequences.
- Do it right away. The sooner you address the problem, the less it has a chance to grow and affect other people and issues.
- If you feel you must make the trickster's actions public, inform him or her that you intend to do so.

## Exercise 9.5

1. When was the last time someone played a dirty trick on you? What did the person say or do?

 ______________________________________________

 ______________________________________________

2. How did you feel? How did you respond?

 ______________________________________________

 ______________________________________________

3. How could you have handled the situation more positively?

 ______________________________________________

 ______________________________________________

# Chapter Checkpoints

✓ A competitive strategy focuses on satisfying one's own interests, often at the expense of others' interests.

✓ There are four common tactics people use to compete: one-upmanship, frontal attack, sabotage, and dirty tricks.

✓ In countering competitive tactics, you need to:

- Keep your emotional cool while staying engaged.
- Refocus on your interests and ask if the tactic is worth confronting.
- Do not take competitive tactics personally, even if they are intended to be personal.
- When necessary, confront competitors with a specific description of what you see them doing.
- Press them to agree to ground rules for working more constructively together.

CHAPTER

# 10 Contending with Compromisers

**This chapter will help you to:**

- Understand what motivates compromisers.
- Review common examples of compromiser political tactics.
- Learn positive political countermoves for dealing with compromisers.

## COMPROMISE STRATEGY AND TACTICS

Like collaborators, compromisers enter negotiations looking for a solution that will satisfy their interests and their partners' interests. But there is an important difference between collaborators and compromisers. Collaborators believe that, through positive politics, partners can build a solution that has a high payoff for everyone. Compromisers believe that the size of the payoff is fixed, so their goal is to obtain as much of this payoff as possible without damaging their relationship with their political partners.

Assume that you and your partner both want to bake pies for dinner parties that you are hosting. You have enough filling for two cherry pies and one apple pie, but only enough dough for one pie. Your partner has just the opposite problem—he has enough dough for three pies, but only enough filling for one apple pie. The collaborator would suggest that together you bake four pies, then divide them between you for your dinner parties. The compromiser would suggest that you bake a cherry pie while he bakes an apple pie, and then he would haggle with you over how much of each pie the two of you should get for your dinner parties. Compromisers believe in a "fixed pie" world. Collaborators believe that it is possible to "grow the pie." ■



Because compromisers believe in a fixed-pie world, they do not believe that it is possible for all partners to fully satisfy their interests in a political situation. Therefore, compromisers employ political tactics that will get them the biggest possible share of the pie without severely damaging their working relationship with others. Contrast this with the political tactics of collaborators, who focus on growing the pie—that is, on creating a pie that is big enough to fully satisfy everyone involved in the negotiations.

## Exercise 10.1

**Think of the compromisers you have known. What were some of the attitudes, beliefs, and fears that turned them into compromisers?**

______________________________________________

______________________________________________

______________________________________________

**In the continuing story of Chris and Charlie, note how Deanna's compromise suggestions fail to satisfy Chris's interests.**

### Shipping and the Surly Sales Representative: Part VIII

Deanna invited Chris to her office to discuss ways of solving the shipping problems that were aggravating Charlie's clients. "Chris, thanks for meeting with me. I know that Charlie can be difficult to work with. I know he doesn't submit his orders on time. I know the orders are difficult to read. But he's an outstanding sales rep, so I'm committed to helping him and you straighten out this shipping problem."

Deanna continued, "I spoke with Charlie this morning, and we think we have a new solution that will work well for everyone. Charlie's sales are growing very rapidly, so he's decided to hire an assistant to help him serve his customers. Charlie said his assistant could process the customer orders every day, then fax them to you right away."

"That sounds great," Chris said.

"Now, because this assistant's primary responsibility will be processing orders, and that's really Shipping's job, Charlie thinks that Shipping should pay the assistant's salary. With taxes and benefits, that would come to about $25,000 per year. Would that be acceptable to you?"

Chris knew that she did not have any money budgeted for this. "Deanna, that hardly seems fair for Shipping to pay for a Sales employee. If she's working for Charlie, then I think Sales should pay her salary."

Deanna was silent for several seconds. "I see your point," she finally said. "I agree, it may be unfair for Shipping to pay her full salary. So let me tell you what I'm prepared to do. I can probably find half the money in my budget. If you're willing to pay the other half of the assistant's salary, I think we can put the shipping problems behind us. Is that a fair compromise?'' ■

As their conversation began, Deanna appeared to offer Chris a deal that would satisfy everyone's interests. But there was a catch—a very expensive catch, from Chris's perspective. Deanna probably did not expect Chris to agree to pay the full salary of the assistant. So Deanna is prepared with a compromise suggestion: What if Chris paid just half the assistant's salary? Compared to paying the full salary, that sounds like a pretty terrific deal, doesn't it? Deanna's compromise will save Chris $12,500, right?

Deanna is using a classic compromise tactic—outrageous demands. Three other tactics often used by compromisers are limited alternatives, cornering, and last-minute add-on requests. Techniques for recognizing and countering compromise tactics are described below.

## OUTRAGEOUS DEMANDS

### Recognizing Outrageous demands

Deanna is using the outrageous demands tactic. She has suggested a solution that is clearly unacceptable to Chris—a solution that Deanna never expects Chris to accept. Then Deanna "generously" reduces her demands. She hopes that a grateful Chris will accept the new compromise solution. Of course, the compromise solution is still skewed in the sales department's favor. It allows it to hire an employee at half price, and it gives Shipping no control over this employee's duties and responsibilities. If Deanna had suggested this solution immediately, Chris would have rejected it out of hand. But as a "compromise" solution, it may sound pretty good to Chris.



### Countering Outrageous Demands

Your first reaction to an outrageous demand might be, "How am I ever going to satisfy this person's interests?" It is certainly good to be concerned about the other person's interests. But the key is to remember that you have interests too!

The following countermoves will help you deal with outrageous demands:

**1. Remember your interests.** Will the compromise solution satisfy your interests? If not, then it is not a good deal for you.

**2. Acknowledge that the outrageous demand is a possible solution.** If you reject the compromise solution out of hand, you risk polarizing your negotiations. Treat it like you would treat any other suggestion. For example, Chris can tell Deanna, "Yes, that's a possible solution. And I appreciate your offer to pay half the assistant's salary. Let's look at ways that we can turn this into a solution that will work for both of us." Then review whether the outrageous demand will satisfy everyone's interests. When it is clear that the demand will not satisfy your interests, ask your partner, "How can we modify your solution so that it meets both our needs?"

**3. Identify benchmarks.** Ask what independent benchmarks your partner used to develop his or her solution. When "compromise" solutions are exposed to objective, independent benchmarks, it often becomes clear that they are almost as outrageous as the initial demands.

**4. Be prepared with your insurance policy.** Remember, one of the two goals of politics is to arrive at a solution that satisfies as many of your interests as possible. A bad agreement that satisfies none of your interests may be far worse than your insurance policy, which satisfies at least some of your interests. Compare the compromise solution to the coverage in your insurance policy (see Chapter 4). If your insurance policy is better, stick with it.



## Exercise 10.2

1. When was the last time a political partner presented you with outrageous demands? What did your partner say or do?

 ______________________________

 ______________________________

2. How did you respond to the demands? Did you consider how they would satisfy (or fail to satisfy) your interests?

 ______________________________

 ______________________________

3. How could you have handled the situation more positively?

 ______________________________

 ______________________________

# LIMITED ALTERNATIVES

## Recognizing Limited Alternatives

To demonstrate their flexibility and willingness to accommodate others, compromisers often offer several potential solutions to their partners. "Let's discuss these. Which one meets your needs best?" they ask. Of course, all of the possible solutions are skewed in their favor. By limiting alternatives to those they have developed, they ensure that they will get everything they want.

If your political partner offers you a choice of alternative solutions, thank him or her. But if your partner fails to ask you for your suggestions, warning bells and sirens should sound in your brain. Your partner may be attempting to limit negotiations to personally favorable alternatives.

## Countering Limited Alternatives

The key to countering limited alternatives is straightforward enough: Make sure you have an opportunity to brainstorm solutions yourself. Here are some pointers:



**1. Do not get drawn into evaluating your partner's alternative solutions.** When your partner presents his solutions, thank him for his hard work. Tell him, "I'm interested in learning more about your ideas. But before we get started weighing the pros and cons of your suggestions, I would like an opportunity to offer my own ideas. And if you have additional ideas, I'd like to hear them, too. The more alternatives we have on the table, the better our final agreement is likely to be." If you start evaluating and building solutions based on your partner's suggestions, you will forfeit your opportunity to make suggestions of your own.

**2. Develop possible solutions in advance of negotiations.** If you suspect that your partner will be preparing possible solutions in advance of your negotiations, it would be wise for you to come prepared with alternatives of your own. Even though you may not fully understand your partner's interests, try to develop solutions that will satisfy his interests as well as yours.

**3. Create time for brainstorming.** At the beginning of your negotiations, suggest that you set aside time to brainstorm solutions together. Your partner may want to generate possible solutions on his own—and that's OK. But suggest that you also brainstorm together. You may be able to create solutions together that neither of you would have considered individually.

### Exercise 10.3

1. When was the last time a political partner presented you with a limited set of alternatives? What did this individual say or do?

   ______________________________

   ______________________________

2. How did you respond to your partner? Did you have an opportunity to suggest your own solutions?

   ______________________________

   ______________________________

3. How could you have handled this situation more positively?

   ______________________________

   ______________________________

# CORNERING

## Recognizing Cornering



Compromisers often try to paint you into a corner—for example, they might say, "This is my best and final offer; take it or leave it"; or "I absolutely have to have a decision by noon today or my offer is withdrawn." Or to strengthen his or her bargaining position, your partner may avoid negotiating with you until the day when you absolutely need to have an agreement.

Compromisers who use the cornering tactic try to pressure you into accepting an agreement that will leave them with a bigger piece of the pie. They hope you will decide that an agreement that offers you a little of what you want is better than no agreement at all.

## Countering Cornering

How can you negotiate with a compromiser who attempts to corner you into an argument? The following countermoves will help:

1. **Stay focused on your interests.** Do not allow your partner's cornering tactics to throw you off balance. Compare your partner's offer with your interests. Which interests does the offer satisfy? Which interests need to be discussed? You will not be able to negotiate with your partner unless you have identified and can explain your concerns.

2. **Find out why your partner is cornering you.** There may be legitimate reasons why your partner is cornering you. Find out why.

3. **Explore possible solutions together.** Once you begin to understand your partner's interests, you can explore possible solutions together.

4. **Insist on fair ground rules for the negotiations.** If the first three countermoves fail, try naming the game. Tell your partner that the tactics he or she is using do not seem fair to you. Ask your partner how it would feel if you used these tactics. Ask what principles the two of you should be using in your negotiations.

It is difficult to like someone who is painting you into a corner, and you may feel like abandoning the negotiations out of spite. Remember, however, that positive politics does not require you to like your partner. It merely requires you to negotiate agreements together effectively. If your countermoves allow you to do that, then your negotiations with the compromiser who is cornering you may help you satisfy many of your interests.



## Exercise 10.4

1. When was the last time someone tried to paint you into a corner during negotiations? What did your partner say or do?

   ______________________________

   ______________________________

2. How did you respond to your partner's behavior?

   ______________________________

   ______________________________

3. How could you have handled the situation more positively?

   ______________________________

   ______________________________

# LAST-MINUTE ADD-ON REQUESTS

## Recognizing Last-Minute Add-On Requests

Some compromisers will wait until an agreement has been reached and then spring "one more thing" on you.

Those who use the add-on tactic hope that you will be so invested in your agreement that you will readily agree to concede a little more. They trust that the goodwill that has been created during negotiations will allow them to slip a little something extra into the agreement.

## Countering Last-Minute Add-On Requests

Add-on requests may leave you with an unpleasant taste in your mouth. You feel that you are being taken advantage of, but you are not sure it is worth the effort of negotiating a whole new agreement with your partner. Here are four pointers that will help you deal with add-ons:

1. **Agree only to a complete agreement.** Until an agreement is final, you cannot be sure whether it will satisfy your interests. You can prevent add-ons by letting your partner know during negotiations that you will agree only to a complete agreement. If your partner asks you to commit to some of the points of the agreement before negotiating final details, say no. An incomplete agreement leaves you open to last-minute surprises.



2. **Determine if the add-on will cost you anything.** If your partner asks for an add-on after a complete agreement has been reached, determine if the add-on will conflict with your interests. If it does not, then accept it.

3. **Reopen negotiations.** If the add-on will require you to sacrifice your interests, let your partner know that your agreement is null and void. For example, you can say, "I'm sorry, but I cannot agree to your request because it will create problems for me. Let's see if we can create a new agreement that solves those problems and satisfies both our interests." The compromiser will withdraw the request when it appears that the add-on will cost something.

4. **Name the tactic.** If your partner uses the add-on tactic often, name the game—for example, "The last four times we have reached an agree-

ment, you have come back later and asked me to do more for you. Could you tell me why you are doing this?" Explain that this tactic makes you reluctant to negotiate agreements in the future.

## Exercise 10.5

1. When was the last time a political partner made an add-on request after you had reached an agreement? What did your partner say or do?

   ______________________________

   ______________________________

2. How did you respond to your partner's request?

   ______________________________

   ______________________________

3. How could you have handled the situation more positively?

   ______________________________

   ______________________________

# Chapter Checkpoints

✓ Compromisers' political goal is to obtain as much of that payoff as possible without jeopardizing their working relationships.

✓ Four of the most common political tactics employed by compromisers are outrageous demands, limited alternatives, cornering, and last-minute add-on requests.

✓ When negotiating with compromisers, it is important to name and challenge their games and insist on fairness.

CHAPTER

# 11 Your Positive Political Campaign

**This chapter will help you to:**

- Analyze your current political "*ALOT*ment."
- Develop a political agenda for the next 90 days.
- Examine the network of relationships that you will need to build or to maintain to achieve your agenda.

In his outstanding book, *The Leadership Factor* (New York: Free Press, 1988), John Kotter reports that a successful leader can be distinguished from a less successful one by his or her **agenda** and his or her **network.**

An agenda is a clear view of what you want to accomplish through your organization during a particular time period. Since you usually need others to achieve your agenda, you must build a network of relationships with people who will work with you to do so.

This view of leadership is very similar to positive politics. Positive politics is about getting the results you want—your agenda—and building strong working relationships with others—your network.

One way to increase the impact of your leadership at work *and* practice the skills in this book is to develop a campaign plan that you can implement in the next 90 days. A positive political campaign plan is a strategy for achieving your agenda while building a strong network of working relationships with people whose support you need.

# YOUR CURRENT POLITICAL POSITION

Your campaign plan for the next 90 days needs to be grounded in a clear understanding of where you stand today. One approach to assessing your current political position is to analyze your *ALOT*ment. It is made up of your political **A**ssets, **L**iabilities, **O**pportunities, and **T**hreats.

Your political **assets** are what you bring to the campaign that will help you achieve your agenda. Your political assets might include a clear idea about what you want to accomplish, skills in persuasion and debate, emotional composure under pressure, powerful allies, access to critical information, a key job or position in your organization, or expertise needed to solve pressing organizational problems.

Your political **liabilities** are things that have the potential to weaken your ability to influence others and achieve your agenda. These liabilities could include the lack of any of the assets above. Or your liabilities might be things such as a reputation as being hard to work with, a tendency to become competitive under pressure, or a poor understanding of the key players and their interests.

Political **opportunities** are situations that are ripe for you to influence in a positive way. Opportunities could include important projects that have floundered for lack of leadership, needed improvements in your organization, new or strengthened relationships with valuable allies, or chances to gain control or access to more resources or information.

Political **threats** are challenges from people or circumstances that may weaken your influence if you do not take action to address them. Examples of threats would include deteriorating relationships with influential people; downward trends in your own or your group's performance; reorganization plans that would reduce your authority; new technologies, systems, or methods that you do not understand; personnel changes that may affect your ability to get things done; or changes in what your "customers" care about.



The chart on page 117 shows how Chris might analyze her current political ALOTment in her situation with Charlie. If she were building a campaign plan, she would need to broaden this analysis to include all the important issues with which she must deal in the next 90 days.

**Chris's Analysis of Her ALOTment**

| Assets | Liabilities |
|---|---|
| ▪ Manager of a key department<br>▪ Access to customer information that is important to Sales and Manufacturing<br>▪ Emotionally composed under pressure<br>▪ Good active listening skills<br>▪ Tolerant of different personal styles<br>▪ Understands her department's challenges<br>▪ Understands and appreciates the challenges of key players in other related departments<br>▪ Respected by Deanna, Charlie's manager | ▪ Manager of a cost center, not a profit center<br>▪ Has less support from her boss and from higher level management than Charlie does<br>▪ Has less direct access than Charlie does to customer concerns<br>▪ Charlie has a long-standing track record of success as a competitor<br>▪ Eric, her boss, is a weak political ally |
| **Opportunities** | **Threats** |
| ▪ Problems in shipping errors are highly visible—fixing them will provide high-level, positive exposure for Chris and her department<br>▪ New technologies are becoming available that Chris's group could use to improve the accuracy and reliability of their shipping system<br>▪ Process problems like this may open the door to strategic alliance with the Total Quality Group, which seems to have top management's ear right now<br>▪ Building an even stronger relationship with Deanna, who is on the management fast track | ▪ Increasing rate of sales growth is threatening to overload the order-entry and shipping system, thus reducing her group's effectiveness<br>▪ Charlie's political antics have limited the careers of people who have crossed him in the past<br>▪ Morale among Shipping staff appears to be deteriorating, due to the department's recent problems and the increasing sense that their technical skills are becoming obsolete<br>▪ A reorganization threatens to move her group under Manufacturing, thus reducing Chris's authority and position in the organizational hierarchy |

## Exercise 11.1

In the table below, write your current political assets, liabilities, opportunities, and threats. Be sure to focus on those things that will be particularly important during the next 90 days.

**Your Current Political ALOTment**

| Assets | Liabilities |
|---|---|
| ▪ | ▪ |
| ▪ | ▪ |
| ▪ | ▪ |
| ▪ | ▪ |
| ▪ | ▪ |
| ▪ | ▪ |
| **Opportunities** | **Threats** |
| ▪ | ▪ |
| ▪ | ▪ |
| ▪ | ▪ |
| ▪ | ▪ |
| ▪ | ▪ |
| ▪ | ▪ |

11

# YOUR 90-DAY POLITICAL AGENDA

Next, determine what key goals you intend to achieve during your 90-day campaign. Since this is a political campaign and politics is about people trying to influence each other, focus your agenda on results that will require joint, cooperative action with other people in your workplace.

To be really motivating, your agenda needs to be made up of SMART goals. A SMART goal is one that is **s**pecific, **m**easurable, **a**greed upon, **r**ealistic, and **t**ime-bound.

For example, Chris's political agenda might include a goal to "Eliminate all shipping errors related to poor communication between the shipping department and field sales during the next 90 days."

This goal is **specific** and **measurable** because it is focused on a single, objective performance factor—shipping errors due to poor communications between two departments. To meet the **agreed-upon** criterion of SMART goals, Chris probably will need Eric, her manager, and all of her subordinates to agree to this goal. Although it may be difficult to achieve, the goal seems **realistic**—and very important. Finally, it is **time-bound** because she intends to make this happen during the next 90-day period.

## Exercise 11.2

What goals are the foundation of your 90-day campaign agenda? Be sure to ask yourself if each goal is SMART.

**Your 90-Day Political Campaign Agenda**

**Goal #1:** ______________________________

______________________________

______________________________

______________________________

______________________________

**Goal #2:** ______________________________

______________________________

______________________________

______________________________

______________________________

*(continued)*

**Your 90-Day Political Campaign Agenda (*concluded*)**

**Goal #3:** ____________________

## BUILDING YOUR POLITICAL NETWORK

The next step is to identify the people who will be most influential in determining whether you achieve your goals. This network may be people you work with all the time or people with whom you do not have much current contact. In the latter case, you may want to consider investing more time in building your relationships with them.

### Identifying Your Political Influentials

#### Exercise 11.3

For each of your three campaign goals write in the squares below the names of three or four people who will be influential in determining whether you are successful in achieving each goal. It is possible that some of the same people will be influential for more than one goal.

**YOUR 90-DAY POLITICAL NETWORKS**

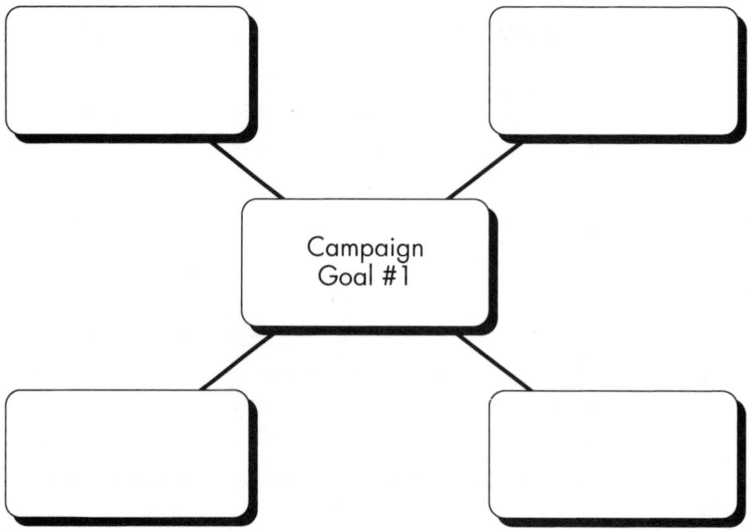

**YOUR 90-DAY POLITICAL NETWORKS *(concluded)***

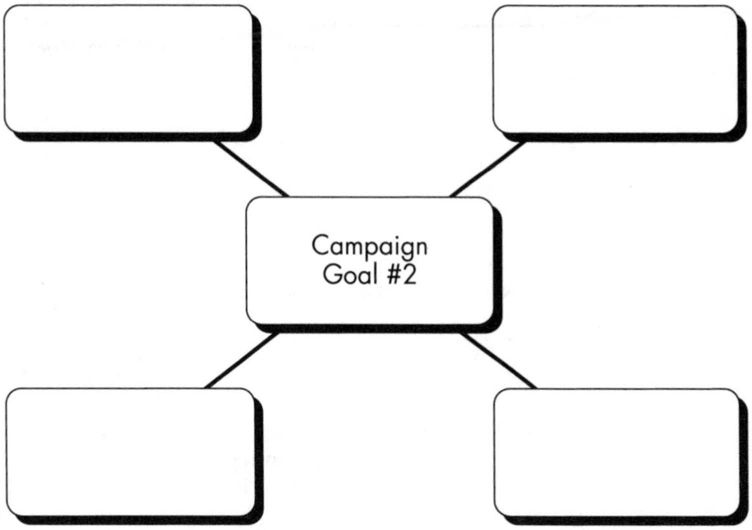


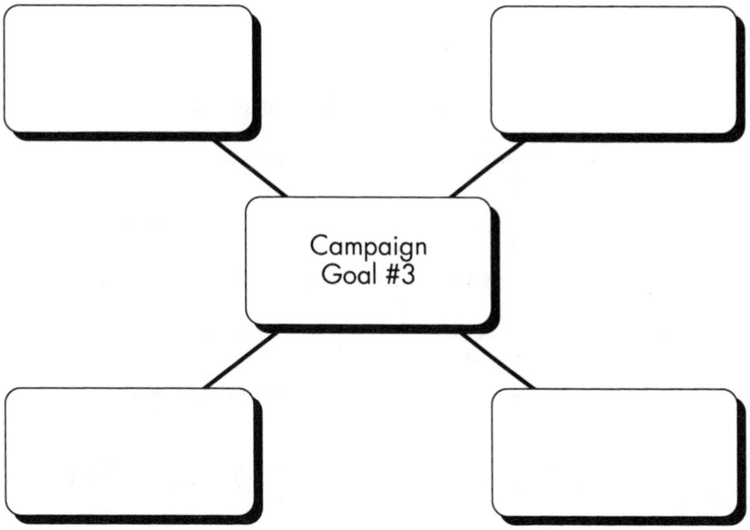


In planning how you will go about building or maintaining these networks of "influentials," evaluate the nature and quality of the relationships you currently have with them.

## Exercise 11.4

Identify the three people in your political network who are likely to have the most impact on your ability to achieve your goals. Write their names in the columns labeled "Influential #1," "Influential #2," and "Influential #3" in the table on page 122, and fill in the empty boxes.

**ASSESSMENT OF CURRENT WORKING RELATIONSHIPS WITH YOUR INFLUENTIALS**

| | **Example:** Charlie | **Influential #1** | **Influential #2** | **Influential #3** |
|---|---|---|---|---|
| *What is the overall quality of this relationship?* | Fair to poor | | | |
| *How often do you interact?* | Weekly | | | |
| *How much do the two of you agree on key issues related to your goals?* | Low agreement | | | |
| *What have been your influential's political strategy and favored tactics to date?* | Competitive: One-upmanship and frontal attack | | | |
| *What have been your political strategy and favored tactics to date?* | Accommodation: Let's play nice | | | |
| *How much investment will you have to make to maintain or improve this relationship?* | A lot of time and a significant amount of emotional energy | | | |
| *What is the likely return on your investment in this relationship?* | Potentially high | | | |

11

## Building Relationships with Your Influentials

Having assessed the quality and nature of your relationships with these three key people, it is time to make some commitments for maintaining and improving these relationships during your 90-day positive politics campaign. Keep these goals as simple as possible.

### Exercise 11.5

For each of your influentials, answer the following questions in the spaces provided.

**CAMPAIGN COMMITMENTS FOR IMPROVING WORK RELATIONSHIPS**

**Influential #1:** ____________________

What have you been doing in this relationship that has been effective? What should you continue to do over the next 90 days?

______________________________________

______________________________________

______________________________________

______________________________________

What have you been doing in this relationship that has been ineffective? What do you need to stop doing, start doing, or do differently over the next 90 days?

______________________________________

______________________________________

______________________________________

______________________________________

**Influential #2:** ____________________

What have you been doing in this relationship that has been effective? What should you continue to do over the next 90 days?

______________________________________

______________________________________

______________________________________

______________________________________

What have you been doing in this relationship that has been ineffective? What do you need to stop doing, start doing, or do differently over the next 90 days?

______________________________________

______________________________________

______________________________________

______________________________________

*(continued)*

**CAMPAIGN COMMITMENTS FOR IMPROVING WORK RELATIONSHIPS**
***(concluded)***

**Influential #3:** ______________________________

What have you been doing in this relationship that has been effective? What should you continue to do over the next 90 days?

______________________________________________________________

______________________________________________________________

______________________________________________________________

______________________________________________________________

What have you been doing in this relationship that has been ineffective? What do you need to stop doing, start doing, or do differently over the next 90 days?

______________________________________________________________

______________________________________________________________

______________________________________________________________

______________________________________________________________

# THE LAST WORD

It is unfortunate that workplace politics has such a negative reputation. It is certainly true that negative politics can be destructive. But there *is* a constructive political alternative: *positive politics*. Positive politics can help people within an organization achieve results *and* build relationships. Positive politics are necessary in the workplace because people need a process for addressing their differences. An organization in which people are asked to keep quiet about their ideas, feelings, and opinions for the "sake of the team" will have a hard time surviving in the turbulent 1990s. Creative adaptation requires a free-flowing climate in which differences of opinion are allowed to flourish.

Fortunately, there is a natural safety factor built into the methods of positive politics. Over time, people who "pretend" to be playing positive politics to exploit others will be detected. We believe that positive politics will triumph over negative politics in the long term. If you are to be successful in your organization over the long run and if you want to feel good about yourself and your achievements, positive politics is your best—and only—option. If you are sincere in your efforts to get results and build relationships, the long-term payoff to you, your co-workers, and your organization will be immeasurable.

# Chapter Checkpoints

✓ Positive politics is a skill and an attitude that develops only when you practice it in real-life situations.

✓ Successful leaders have an agenda and a network of relationships to help them implement their agenda.

✓ Following through on your 90-day positive political campaign is the best way to practice your new skills and increase your political influence in your organization.

✓ Sincerity is critical to making positive politics work for you, your co-workers, and your organization.

# Post-Test

Answer the following questions to test your understanding of the key ideas in this book. Circle the letter that best answers each question. Answers appear on page 129.

**1.** Politics in the workplace is:

**A.** A sign that an organization is in real trouble.

**B.** The result of a lack of leadership.

**C.** Avoided by people who are truly effective.

**D.** The result of people having different opinions, attitudes, values, and interests.

**2.** Which of the following is *not* one of the tests you should use in deciding whether to fight a political battle?

**A.** Are my needs and interests at stake?

**B.** What is my probability of success?

**C.** Do I trust the person I am at odds with?

**D.** What is the priority of this particular battle?

**3.** Which political strategy is highly assertive and uncooperative?

**A.** Avoidance.

**B.** Accommodation.

**C.** Competition.

**D.** Compromise.

**4.** Which of the following is *not* one of the four positive steps for getting results?

**A.** Identify issues, solutions, and interests.

**B.** Take out a political insurance policy.

**C.** Give in on minor points to get negotiations started.

**D.** Look for benchmarks.

**5.** Which of the following is *not* an example of how to empower others to choose for themselves?

**A.** Attacking the problem, not the person.

**B.** Thinking and talking about the logic of different solutions.

**C.** Exploring a wide variety of possible solutions.

**D.** Committing to a solution early in negotiations.

**6.** Which of the following is a poor example of how to name the negative tactic that your political partner is using?

**A.** "You've failed to keep three commitments you made to me. Could you please explain what is preventing you from keeping these commitments?"

**B.** "You seem angry about something I am doing. I suggest we end this meeting so you can cool down."

**C.** "You are very quiet today. Will you please share your thoughts with me?"

**D.** "I've heard from several people that you've been criticizing me behind my back. Would you please tell me why you're doing this?"

**7.** What is the avoider's motto?

**A.** "Things can only get worse."

**B.** "I want everyone to be happy."

**C.** "There's too much conflict in this world."

**D.** "If you scratch my back, I'll scratch yours."

**8.** Which of the following is *not* an accommodation political tactic?

**A.** One-upmanship.

**B.** Obsequiousness.

**C.** Smile-and-denial.

**D.** Martyrdom.

**9.** "I don't know why we even listen to your suggestions after the way you messed up the First City Bank project last week" is an example of which tactic?

**A.** One-upmanship.

**B.** Frontal attack.

**C.** Sabotage.

**D.** Dirty tricks.

**10.** Which of the following best describes the compromiser's political goal?

**A.** Ensuring that everyone's needs are satisfied.

**B.** Keeping the peace between the organization's most powerful politicians.

**C.** Skewing the outcome in his or her own favor.

**D.** Maintaining positive relationships with co-workers.

**11.** To create a political campaign plan, you will need to:

**A.** Understand your political ALOTment.

**B.** Develop a 90-day political agenda.

**C.** Examine your network of relationships.

**D.** Do all of the above.

ANSWER KEY

| | | | | |
|---|---|---|---|---|
| 1. **D** | 2. **C** | 3. **C** | 4. **C** | 5. **D** |
| 6. **B** | 7. **A** | 8. **A** | 9. **B** | 10. **C** |
| 11. **D** | | | | |

# THE BUSINESS SKILLS EXPRESS SERIES

This growing series of books addresses a broad range of key business skills and topics to meet the needs of employees, human resource departments, and training consultants.

To obtain information about these and other Business Skills Express books, please call Business One IRWIN toll free at: 1-800-634-3966.

| | |
|---|---|
| Effective Performance Management | ISBN 1-55623-867-3 |
| Hiring the Best | ISBN 1-55623-865-7 |
| Writing that Works | ISBN 1-55623-856-8 |
| Customer Service Excellence | ISBN 1-55623-969-6 |
| Writing for Business Results | ISBN 1-55623-854-1 |
| Powerful Presentation Skills | ISBN 1-55623-870-3 |
| Meetings that Work | ISBN 1-55623-866-5 |
| Effective Teamwork | ISBN 1-55623-880-0 |
| Time Management | ISBN 1-55623-888-6 |
| Assertiveness Skills | ISBN 1-55623-857-6 |
| Motivation at Work | ISBN 1-55623-868-1 |
| Overcoming Anxiety at Work | ISBN 1-55623-869-X |
| Positive Politics at Work | ISBN 1-55623-879-7 |
| Telephone Skills at Work | ISBN 1-55623-858-4 |
| Managing Conflict at Work | ISBN 1-55623-890-8 |
| The New Supervisor: Skills for Success | ISBN 1-55623-762-6 |
| The *Americans with Disabilities Act*: What Supervisors Need to Know | ISBN 1-55623-889-4 |